SUCCESSFUL MERGERS

OTHER TITLES FROM
THE ECONOMIST BOOKS

The Economist Desk Companion
The Economist Economics
The Economist Guide to Economic Indicators
The Economist Guide to the European Union
The Economist Numbers Guide
The Economist Style Guide
The Guide to Analysing Companies
The Guide to Business Modelling
The Guide to Financial Markets
The Guide to Management Ideas
The Dictionary of Economics
The International Dictionary of Finance
Business Ethics
E-Commerce
Improving Marketing Effectiveness
Managing Complexity
Measuring Business Performance
Successful Innovation

Pocket Accounting
Pocket Advertising
Pocket Director
Pocket Economist
Pocket Finance
Pocket International Business Terms
Pocket Internet
Pocket Investor
Pocket Law
Pocket Manager
Pocket Marketing
Pocket MBA
Pocket Money
Pocket Negotiator
Pocket Strategy

Pocket Asia
Pocket Europe in Figures
Pocket World in Figures

The
Economist

SUCCESSFUL MERGERS

Marion Devine

THE ECONOMIST IN ASSOCIATION WITH
PROFILE BOOKS LTD

Published by Profile Books Ltd
58A Hatton Garden, London EC1N 8LX

Typeset in EcoType by MacGuru
info@macguru.org.uk

Printed in Great Britain by
St Edmundsbury Press, Bury St Edmunds

A CIP catalogue record for this book is available
from the British Library

ISBN 1 86197 360 8

For information on other Economist Books, visit
www.profilebooks.co.uk
www.economist.com

Contents

Acknowledgements

I am indebted to the companies and individuals who contributed to this book and who generously shared their experiences, both good and bad, of going through a merger. Special thanks to Diageo, particularly Phil Radcliffe, director of strategic change, Stephen Dando, former HR director of Guinness UDV GB, James Tugendhat, commercial director of Guinness UDV, and Simon Lenton, HR director of Guinness UDV GB. Thanks also to the WPP Group, especially Laurence Mellman, director of special projects, Mike Walsh, CEO (Europe, Middle East and Africa) of Ogilvy & Mather, and Michael Madel, president and CEO of J.Walter Thompson (Europe, Middle East & Africa). Two individuals, Michel Syrett, an independent writer, and Stephen Bull, associate partner at Accenture, were always willing to encourage, listen and debate ideas during the writing of the book. Another much appreciated source of practical help is my sister Nuala Bell, who gave invaluable help during school holidays. Many thanks to Stephen Brough, my publisher, for his steady guidance and patience throughout the whole process.

1 Introduction

COMPANIES COME AND GO, chief executives rise and fall, industry sectors wax and wane, but an outstanding feature of the past decade has been the rise of mergers and acquisitions (M&AS).

Whether in times of boom or bust, M&AS continue to be the preferred option for businesses seeking to grow rapidly and, more importantly, change the rules of the game in their sector. M&A activity reached record levels between 1995 and 2000. According to Dealogic, a research firm that specialises in investment banking,[1] the recent M&A wave peaked in 2000, with $3.5 trillion worth of announced bids, compared with $1.9 trillion in 2001.

The value of cross-border activity, especially between America and Europe, increased by 900% during the past decade. Dealogic reported that cross-border activity accounted for 37% of the total global activity in 2001, with a value of $698 billion from 7,669 deals. During 2000, the UK was the most acquisitive country in cross-border M&A deals, spending $337 billion, followed by France ($137 billion) and the United States ($136 billion). During 2001, the United States spent the most on foreign acquisitions ($145 billion). There continues to be a brisk trade between the United States and the UK (see Charts 1.1 and 1.2 on the next page).

In 2001 there was a marked decrease in global M&A activity. The total number of announced (rather than completed) deals was 17.3% lower than in 2000 (24,692 compared with 30,350), according to Dealogic. The most striking difference between 2000 and 2001 is in the size of deals. Although there was a decline in the value of completed deals worth

M&A terminology

M&A is often used as an interchangeable term, a convenient but inaccurate usage. Mergers refer to deals where two or more companies take virtually equal stakes in each other's businesses, whereas an acquisition is the straightforward purchase of a "target" company. M&AS are generally referred to as mergers or combinations in this book, partly for convenience but also because of the focus on how companies can pool their resources and capabilities.

Chart 1.1 **British acquisitions of US targets, 1995–2001**[a]

Year	$ m	Bids
1995	5,387	72
1996	14,965	80
1997	10,497	117
1998	78,872	123
1999	118,213	183
2000	62,572	219
2001	5,043	104

a Excluding withdrawn deals and share buy-backs. Announced deals January 1st 1995–June 18th 2001. Target nationality US; bidder nationality British.
Source: Dealogic

Chart 1.2 **US acquisitions of British targets, 1995–2001**[a]

Year	$ m	Bids
1995	11,417	131
1996	16,779	155
1997	26,101	225
1998	32,262	369
1999	56,875	281
2000	37,007	365
2001	9,616	108

a Excluding withdrawn deals and share buy-backs. Announced deals January 1st 1995–June 18th 2001. Target nationality British; bidder nationality US.
Source: Dealogic

over $10 billion (28 in 2001 compared with 42 in 2000), the market for smaller deals (below $1 billion) remained buoyant (see Chart 1.3).

M&As help big and small players alike. Although it is the "mega deals" that receive much of the media attention, thousands of medium-sized companies, particularly niche players, use acquisitions to help them develop their specialist and innovative capabilities.

In the *Harvard Business Review* in 2000,[2] Alex Mandl, chairman and chief executive of Teligent, an American provider of voice, data and Internet services to small to medium-sized businesses, commented:

Chart 1.3 **Value bands of global completed deals, 2000 and 2001**

Value bands	2000 $ bn[a]	2000 Bids	2001 $ bn[a]	2001 Bids	% change
Over $10bn	1,401.3	42	593.0	28	−58
$5bn–10bn	436.7	59	155.0	23	−65
$1bn–5bn	909.0	398	551.1	247	−39
$500m–1bn	313.8	423	207.7	270	−34
$100m–500m	421.5	1,820	315.7	1,363	−25
$50m–100m	97.9	1,307	76.2	926	−22
Less than $50m	126.7	10,380	90.4	8,126	−29
Total	**3,706.9**	**14,429**	**1,989.1**	**10,983**	**−46**

a Total value of completed deals in each value band.
Source: Dealogic

> *Growth through acquisition has been a critical part of the success of many companies operating in the new economy ... The plain fact is that acquiring is much faster than building. And speed – speed to market, speed to positioning, speed to becoming a viable company – is absolutely essential in the new economy.*

Serial acquirers

Many big companies owe much of their success to skilful acquiring. For example, as a global provider of Internet networks, Cisco Systems has used acquisitions as its route to growth. Between 1994 and 2000, it acquired some 50 companies at a cost of around $20 billion. Despite the company's difficulties following the bursting of the technology bubble in 2000 and the ensuing economic downturn, Cisco's chief executive, John Chambers, remains robustly committed to acquisitions:

> *If each time a hesitation occurs in the market and the company pulls back on inventory and [does] not have an aggressive acquisition strategy, then we can't be the major company that we are today. We take calculated risks and we are not going to change that.*

In future, Cisco will take a more cautious approach to acquisitions: "It (Cisco's acquisition strategy) absolutely works to our benefit. Are we going to be more selective? Yes. Will we wait longer? Yes."
Other American-based "serial acquirers" include:

- General Electric, which during 1996–2000 made over 100 acquisitions a year. GE, however, may not have the same appetite for acquisitions given its unsuccessful attempt to merge with Honeywell during 2001. In the process of investigating the merger, the EU's Merger Task Force focused attention on GE's dominance of European aerospace markets.
- AT&T, a telecommunications group, which has spent $100 billion on acquisitions since 1998, acquiring, for example, MediaOne in 1999.
- Microsoft, a software giant, which is reputed to have $50 billion available for acquisitions. The company buys on average ten technology companies a year, and has acquired a total of 51 companies since 1995. Microsoft's approach is to invest in businesses that provide software services and solutions, such as systems integrators, as well as "demand generation" companies, such as Internet service providers, that help to encourage the adoption of Microsoft technologies. The company's third preference is for companies developing emerging technologies. During 2001, for example, it used acquisitions to strengthen its presence in the computer-games market.

European "serial acquirers" include:

- CRH, a building materials group based in Ireland. The group relies on what it terms its "bolt-on acquisition strategy" to help increase its presence in 19 countries. CRH typically buys small, often family-owned, building companies. During 2000, it acquired 60 businesses, at a cost of €1.6 billion ($10.3 billion), and the following year it spent €1 billion ($1.15 billion) on acquiring 22 businesses.
- WPP, a global advertising group, has a remarkable M&A track record, having merged with leading advertising agencies including Ogilvy & Mather, J. Walter Thompson and Young & Rubicam. According to Dealogic, the group agreed 27 deals in 2001, making it the UK's most acquisitive company that year. The

group made news of a slightly different kind when it tried to wriggle out of its $491m bid to buy Tempus, an international media-buying group, in late 2001. Sir Martin Sorrell, WPP's CEO, argued unsuccessfully to the British Takeover Panel that WPP should be allowed to withdraw from the deal because there had been a "material adverse change" in Tempus's prospects following the September 11th terrorist attacks in America. His case was not helped by the fact that WPP had bought shares in Tempus after that fateful day. Tempus is now part of WPP.

Laurence Mellman, WPP's director of special projects, is responsible for overseeing the group's acquisitions. He comments:

> We strongly encourage our operating companies to make their own acquisitions. We might be looking for growth of 15–20%. In a good year, organic growth might account for an average 8–10% growth, leaving a gap. We have to fill the gap through acquisitions. So we push our people to acquire. Probably on average, we are looking for growth of 7–10% from acquisitions and the same for organic growth.

Mr Mellman stresses that the most valuable assets that WPP gains through mergers are people.

> WPP's entrepreneurial culture is helped by the type of people who have joined the group through acquisitions. Many of them were running their own company before they joined us. So an entrepreneurial style of management is perpetuated in the company.

Clifford Chance, a leading law firm, also emphasises the "intellectual assets" that can be gained through mergers. The firm broke new ground in its sector by using acquisitions as a fast track towards global legal practice. In January 2000, Clifford Chance completed a merger with Pünder, a German firm, and Rogers & Wells, an American firm. Michael Bray, the new firm's CEO, declares:

> A merger is an enormous catalyst. It creates an environment in which we can change and redefine the way we do things. In Clifford Chance, we have found ourselves specialising more

Chart 1.4 **M&As by industry sector, 1995–2001**

Industry sector	1995		1996		1997		1998	
	$bn	Bids	$bn	Bids	$bn	Bids	$bn	Bids
Telecommunications	90.6	409	162.2	551	237.4	743	362.1	927
Broadcasting & telecommunication	90.6	409	162.2	551	237.4	743	362.1	927
Finance & insurance	154.5	1,104	150.3	1,229	376.9	1,836	404.9	2,417
Credit intermediation & related authorities	83.3	476	55.5	516	184.0	804	234.3	931
Insurance carriers & related activities	40.7	266	62.9	321	89.0	459	103.7	634
Paper, printing, metal & machinery	82.2	1,335	74.3	1,609	135.8	2,158	333.0	2,650
Machinery manufacturing	6.0	281	7.8	363	21.5	424	25.0	535
Petroleum & coal products manufacturing	4.6	26	6.1	38	16.2	78	139.5	69
Transportation equipment manufacturing	18.1	221	22.2	239	21.6	341	71.3	400
Media, information & software	66.0	632	43.8	966	55.0	1,667	113.2	2,583
Publishing industries	21.6	342	25.0	444	26.5	770	46.7	950
Computer systems design and related services	5.9	169	9.1	323	13.6	438	33.3	820
Information services & data processing services	29.2	69	7.6	122	5.5	346	10.4	638
Chemicals & pharmaceuticals	61.9	573	66.0	628	65.6	861	130.4	1,117
Chemical manufacturing	54.1	394	60.9	429	56.6	644	115.2	841
Plastics & rubber products manufacturing	7.8	179	5.0	199	9.0	217	15.2	276

Source: Dealogic

and more ... but the new firm can learn from Pünder, where partners often combine specialist expertise with an ability to advise over a broad range of matters. We can also learn from Rogers & Wells, where the practice areas are broader, as in many US firms. We need to cross-fertilise the best of these systems.

1999		2000		2001		Total	
$bn	*Bids*	*$bn*	*Bids*	*$bn*	*Bids*	*$bn*	*Bids*
620.5	1,604	769.4	2,223	116.1	582	2,358.2	7,039
620.5	1,604	769.4	2,223	116.1	582	2,358.2	7,039
452.8	2,868	531.8	2,852	208.8	1,056	2,279.9	13,362
248.9	1,067	224.8	963	122.4	334	1,153.1	5,091
105.0	670	115.4	611	49.4	249	566.2	3,210
419.4	2,942	225.5	2,681	85.0	1,016	1,355.2	14,391
208.3	597	30.2	545	7.0	219	305.8	2,964
33.0	111	51.0	117	24.2	44	274.6	483
69.0	453	49.2	411	6.9	156	258.3	2,221
163.8	4,166	388.7	6,203	36.4	1,551	866.9	17,768
57.5	1,107	93.6	1,131	9.2	359	280.1	5,103
44.9	1,731	113.4	2,976	17.4	697	237.7	7,154
53.7	1,114	70.6	1,856	6.4	404	183.3	4,549
298.8	1,177	179.2	1,156	26.9	426	828.7	5,938
281.0	882	166.9	867	24.3	339	758.9	4,396
17.8	295	12.3	289	2.6	87	69.8	1,542

Sectors compared

Since the mid-1990s, M&As have acted as powerful catalysts of change. Based on the total value of deals since 1995, the sectors with the most M&A activity are shown in Chart 1.4. They are:

- telecommunications: deals totalled $2,358 billion. The peak year was 2000, when 2,223 deals were completed, worth $769 billion;

- finance and insurance: deals totalled $2,280 billion. These peaked in 2000, when 2,852 deals were completed, worth $532 billion;
- paper, printing metal and machinery: deals totalled $1,355 billion, reaching a high in 1999 of 2,942 deals, worth $419 billion;
- media, information and software: deals totalled $867 billion, with a surge in 2000 when 6,203 transactions were completed, worth $389 billion;
- chemicals and pharmaceuticals: deals totalled $829 billion. The volume of deals peaked in 1999 with 1,177 transactions, worth $299 billion.

Through M&As industry sectors are restructuring to create new linkages. For example, in the last five years there has been a fusion between media providers and specialists in Internet services and software. As Steve Case, chairman, said of the AOL Time Warner merger, completed in 2001 (see also "M&A insights" below):

> We didn't do our merger simply to achieve our 2001 objectives. We did this merger because we think we are at the right place, at the right time, with the right management, the right brands and the right technology assets. We have the wind at our back, as the world moves ... to be a more converged, interactive world.

Despite the difficulties in complex mergers, recombining intellectual and tangible assets is often the only way to survive.

M&A INSIGHTS

Steve Case, chairman, AOL Time Warner
"What the last few years have made crystal clear is that rapidly changing, Internet-charged economy companies must constantly reinvent themselves to attract new customers. And today, it is not how many assets your company has, it is how you connect those assets and constantly innovate to serve customers better.

"In this environment, it is critical to integrate the new technologies for consumers. Whether in wireless or other new markets, both individual companies and industries must build bridges between platforms, mediums, content and services – capitalising on new synergies, creating new businesses, and taking advantage of transforming business opportunities.

"That ... is our game plan for AOL Time Warner ... Our combined assets are unrivalled – not only because of their range and value, but because they fit together like pieces of a puzzle. From the world's most popular media, Internet and communications brands and properties, to our technological expertise and infrastructure, we are poised to lead the next wave of growth."[3]

Sold on synergies ...

At the heart of these deals is the notion of "synergies", a much-loved and overworked management phrase. The concept of synergies is sometimes used loosely to describe a mysterious chemistry between combining companies. In fact, the term refers to the combination of various physical, financial and intellectual assets such that their value is greater than the sum of their individual worth. Mercer Delta, a consultancy specialising in "organisation architecture and change", says that fuzzy notions of synergy should be replaced by "hard-nosed concrete descriptions". Its suggested lists of M&A synergies include both tangible and intangible assets, such as:

- corporate brands and well-defined reputation;
- capital and new streams of revenue;
- core competencies in management or business processes;
- people who possess unique skills or customer relationships;
- needed elements of a culture or operating environment;
- management resources.

Many of these assets are people based. Employees at every level of an organisation help to forge a corporate brand identity and reputation. Employees help to create new streams of revenue by being close to the market place and recognising new opportunities. Leaders use various resources to mobilise people's energies towards a set of strategic goals. Talented people contribute their expertise within a supportive and enabling corporate culture.

... some of which aren't easy to achieve

There's the rub. People-based assets are difficult to manage – it is not a simple task to harness people's intellects, emotions and imaginations. Nor is it easy to persuade employees to behave in certain ways or to endorse cherished corporate values. Today's M&A is often like a bucking bronco – the ride can be exciting but the chances of being thrown off are high. As legal transactions, M&As are complex. As organisational and individual events, they are even more difficult. Under intense pressure to perform, companies and individuals often appear to be gripped by temporary insanity, behaving in unpredictable and irrational ways. Getting to grips with both the technical aspects of mergers and their human dimension is a challenging task.

Sir John Reed, CEO of Citicorp, initially viewed a merger as an alignment of "business systems", only to be rudely awakened to the anarchic reality. Following the merger between Citicorp and Travelers Group to create Citigroup, one of the world's largest financial services companies, he confidently predicted in June 1999:

> The culture will take care of itself. People ultimately learn to work together. They may not like it. They may complain a lot. But, you know what? In five years from now, they will be quite surprised at how they have learned to get along.[4]

However, by March 2000 he acknowledged the potency of human behaviour:

> We are talking about putting together two cultures that are quite different, quite distinct. I am trying hard to understand how to make this work. I will tell you that it is not simple and it is not easy, and it is not clear to me that it will necessarily be successful. Just as the human body sometimes rejects an organ that it needs, business systems can sometimes reject behaviours that are required for a system's success.
>
> As you put two cultures together, you get all sorts of strange aberrant behaviour ... the willingness of people to change is limited and what you pay them seems to be inversely correlated to their willingness to change.[5]

Plainly, M&As need to be approached with an open mind, a willingness to be flexible and, above all, humility.

This book looks at M&As as strategic and legal transactions, and also as profoundly human-driven events. To focus on one perspective only is to fail to capture the full complexity of M&As. Any attempt to manage a merger as simply a legal and transactional event will be doomed to failure – well-honed strategies and logical organisational charts fall by the wayside if human beings decide to subvert or sabotage the process. A failure to harness people-based assets will lead to a business that is bigger, but not particularly better.

Perceptions and reality

A gap appears to exist between what experts say about M&As and what managers experience. The interviews of experienced merger managers carried out by the author during 2000 and 2001, as well as extensive trawls of information in the public domain, suggests that few M&A transitions can be neatly packaged into a set of processes, or a single magic formula.

Most M&As are a blend of planning and "seat of the pants" management, with the business and integration strategy being adjusted in the crucible of experience. This is especially true when the external environment is moving at a faster pace than the integration itself. Integration approaches are constantly amended to take into account unpredictable events and unforeseen problems. Organisational charts are rewritten as managers see new opportunities for internal and external synergies. Plans that are sound in theory prove difficult to execute in practice, as managers and employees struggle to alter their behaviour and work together. Managers in the middle of this experience use whatever tool, process or behaviour will get them through to the next stage of integration.

This combination of order and chaos, the planned and the emergent, is the hallmark of almost every M&A. Yet merger studies often hold up a very different mirror. All too often, merger analysis takes place some time after the dust has settled. The merger story is told with the benefit of hindsight. Whether they intend to or not, managers often give sanitised versions of the merger or acquisition. They may forget the daily insights that helped them make the merger work. In an effort to make sense of their experiences, they may imagine or invent an order and logic that was not there at the time.

Although such post-event perspectives are valuable, it seems useful to try to counterbalance stories of past deals with those that are current. This book draws on the existing body of merger literature, but in its attempt to convey the reality it includes snapshots of managers living through demanding integration programmes. Their insights and often painful experiences reveal that merger management is as much an art as a science.

Strategic considerations

What is a truly "transformational" merger? Some of the people interviewed for this book talked hesitantly about their sense that mergers
have the potential to be transformational events, enabling the organisation to achieve a step change in its culture, structure and activities.
Few of the interviewees felt that their M&A had achieved such a
degree of transformation – the magical $1 + 1 = 5$ formula that so many
management consultants like to talk about. In piecing together their
comments and experiences, it became clear that most felt that their
organisations were still failing to tap into their intellectual assets, and
that the enduring challenge of any merger is to knock down internal
barriers and help the merging organisations to pool their intellectual
and emotional capital.

Efforts to tap into the intellectual capabilities of combining organisations have been hampered by a tendency to see people as objects that
can be moved around the organisation at will. M&As are things that are
"done" to people, who can either comply with the process or impede its
execution. Human-resources managers are often excluded from merger
discussions and negotiations, and have few opportunities to persuade
their colleagues to consider the "human element", let alone make it a
core part of the merger strategy. If human-resources managers fail to
make a solid business argument about the contribution that employees
can make to the success or failure of a merger, senior managers typically
push the whole subject to one side, assuming that it can be dealt with on
an ad hoc basis at a later stage. They mistakenly believe that the human
dimension of M&As is the province of the human-resources department
and essentially a post-acquisition, operational issue.

The attitude that people are somehow peripheral to M&As is closely
connected to assumptions about how merger strategy is formulated and
implemented via the acquisition process. Senior managers often assume
that merger success hinges on the uninterrupted flow of purpose and
strategy from the top/centre of the new entity to its most peripheral
operations. Merger managers are under intense pressure to present a
brilliantly conceived strategy, thereby demonstrating their new-found
dynamism. They accordingly announce a strategy that promises a range
of synergies over the short and medium term, and offer it to analysts,
investors and media commentators to pick over during the ensuing
weeks. In reality, such merger strategies are what Henry Mintzberg, a
professor at McGill University, describes as "designed strategy", a grand
intellectual exercise that rests on the idealised concept of management

as a process of planning, organising, commanding and controlling people and resources, rather than, as Mr Mintzberg argues, something that includes improvising, adjusting, fire-fighting, reacting and learning. This last list is a far better description of what happens during a merger. Yet employees typically believe the assertions of their new leaders. Diane Iorfida, executive vice-president and director of worldwide human resources at Leo Burnett, an international advertising agency, says that employees continue to have faith in the idea of a grand plan, even when there is no evidence of its existence:

Employees' expectation is that you have dotted all the Is and crossed all the Ts ... The automatic thinking of most employees is ... that, somewhere, you have a plan and you're not telling them about it.

In reality, a fully formed merger strategy is a myth. Often the management team has merely predicted synergies derived from cost cutting and economies of scale. Most of these synergies are won through the better exploiting of tangible assets. A careful look at some of the promised synergies reveals that they are actually conservative estimates. On the longer-term synergies that can only be achieved through leveraging the new entity's intellectual assets, there is often silence.

For example, during the presentation on the merger between two oil companies, BP and Amoco, the new co-chairman, Sir John Browne, spoke of expected synergies at an annual rate totalling $2 billion (pretax) by the end of 2000. These synergies were based on cost savings in areas such as "organisational efficiency" and rationalisation, more focused exploration and joint procurement. On how the merged company would grow, he was noticeably more vague:

The deal offers the prospect for growth – the opportunity to do more ... and that means we can look forward to a rate of growth for the new company which will go beyond the targets which we (BP) and Amoco have already set out in the last few months. This is the dynamic which a snapshot can't show but which is a vital outcome of this deal.

James Crowley, head of the UK strategy and business architecture division at Accenture, a management and technology services organisation, says that management teams often have an "intuitive" sense of the synergies offered by a merger, but these benefits can be complex and difficult to articulate.

> By the time of a merger announcement, merger teams have an intuitive sense of what the joint business will look like. This intuition is based on judgment, experience and crude numbers. But when it comes to presenting their thoughts to the financial community, they will often talk about synergies that can be quantified and are easy to explain, such as synergies gained through cost reductions, "performance push", where a new injection of management expertise can help drive up margins; and benefits gained from financial engineering, for example taxation benefits. It is much harder to explain and quantify the benefits of a new strategy, or to predict growth achieved through mixing the merged company's capabilities and assets.

Intuition may not seem a valid basis for deciding to merge, but it is nonetheless something that drives many deals. Much of that intuition rests on an awareness that the long-term success of a merger depends on people – their knowledge, expertise, imagination and creativity. This view is expressed eloquently by Ed Smith, who is responsible for global learning and education at PricewaterhouseCoopers, a professional services firm that resulted from a merger between Price Waterhouse and Coopers & Lybrand in June 1998:

> I have a passionate belief that what drives our merged business is the intellectual capacity of our people and their creativity and motivation. If we can harvest and capture that capacity, we release the potential of people.

Intellectually based synergies are achieved through a process that is emergent (using Mr Mintzberg's term again) rather than designed. It is not an easy process, nor is it glamorous. Such synergies do not come from top-down strategy formulation, but through processes that enable people at all levels of the organisation to contribute their ideas and insights. As a result, mergers that yield synergies based on both tangible assets and intellectual assets do so through a combination of designed and emergent strategies. Designed strategy helps to give overall purpose and direction, and emergent strategy helps to push the boundary of that thinking to its limits. Together they are able to form a virtuous circle, where each feeds and renews the other.

Conjuring the magic circle

A company's integration process can ensure the formation of such a circle. It acts rather like the Gulf stream, where the flow of hot and cold water ensures a continuous cyclical movement. A well-designed integration process ensures that the new entity's designed strategy reaches deep into the organisation, ensuring a unity of purpose. Basically, everyone understands the purpose and logic of the deal. The integration process can ensure that ideas and creativity are not dissipated but are fed into the emergent strategy of the organisation. This is achieved through the day-to-day job of encouraging and motivating people, and also creating forums where people can think the impossible. Chart 1.5 on the next page demonstrates the relationship between designed and emergent strategy and merger integration. It suggests how merging organisations can become learning organisations: strategy formulation and implementation merges into collective learning.

Some merger failures can be explained by this model. For example, serious problems arise when a company relies too heavily on designed strategy. If the management team is not getting high-quality feedback and information from the rest of the organisation, it runs the risk of becoming cut off. Employees may perceive their leaders as being out of touch with the reality of the merger, leading to a gradual loss of confidence in the senior management's ability to chart the future of the new entity. Similarly, the leadership team may not receive timely information about external threats, brought about perhaps by the predatory actions of competitors or dissatisfied customers, with the result that performance suffers and the new management is criticised for failing to get to grips with the complexities of the changeover.

However, too much reliance on emergent strategy can lead to the sense of a leadership vacuum within the combining organisations. The management team may seem to lack direction, or to be moving too slow. This often leads to political infighting and territory building, and the departure of many talented people.

Balancing act

A careful balance needs to be struck between designed and emergent strategy in order to ensure that each process feeds into the other. Such a balance requires people to be treated as valuable assets. This challenges

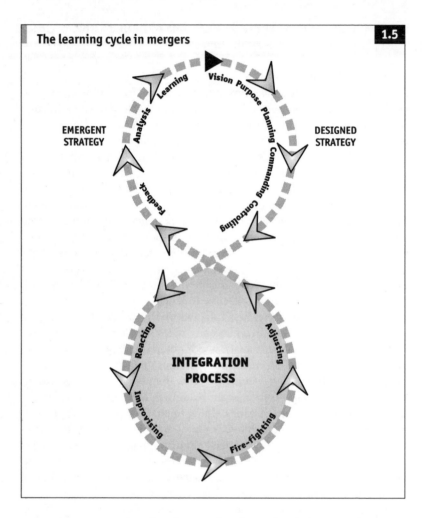

The learning cycle in mergers — 1.5

a common assumption that the people who make mergers work are primarily those with high-status roles such as leading integration teams and task-forces. In reality, a merger works because diverse groups of employees commit themselves to its success and play a vital role in smoothing processes, fine-tuning strategy and even inventing solutions when things do not go to plan.

Some may argue that the model outlined in Chart 1.5 is a symptom of weak management. A more positive interpretation is that it is a sign of strength. Two or more organisations only truly combine when everyone pools their skills, knowledge and imagination. Corporate strategists formulate a strategy and vision that enables the merger to get started. However, that strategy acquires force and resonance when people are given the opportunity to deepen or refine the thinking and assumptions underpinning the strategy. In doing so, more people gain a sense of involvement. They begin to invest energy and emotion into making the deal work.

Lead and involve – and learn

But what about M&As that result in large job losses and site closures? What about hostile deals? Is it really possible to engage employees when so many of them might eventually lose their jobs or go through months of stressful upheaval, only to end up performing similar roles at similar rates of pay? There is no denying that deals involving substantial downsizing are difficult to manage. However, a central argument of this book is that merger leadership makes a crucial difference. Even people who will eventually lose their jobs can be persuaded to help make the deal work. But if managers expect little or nothing of value from the majority of their people they will probably make that expectation a reality. They will overlook opportunities for mutual learning and value creation.

Shell UK, for example, made a painful discovery when senior managers reviewed their experience of integrating Gulf Oil. Shell UK acquired Gulf Oil (GB), a subsidiary of Chevron, in December 1997 and completed its full integration by early 1999. Because most of Chevron's people would not be retained, Shell assumed they would not co-operate during the "lights out" closure programme and excluded them from planning teams. However, Chevron people turned out to be co-operative and were anxious to maintain professional standards to the very end. Shell realised it had missed an opportunity to learn from Chevron. Simon Clare, then head of the retail integration team, commented:

> Ironically, Gulf's way of working was in many ways closer to Shell's vision of the future ... At the time of the acquisition, however, the opportunity to leverage this change through the implementation was not seen as a priority.[6]

The process of involvement and mutual learning can also emerge under the banner of a different process altogether. For example, when Halifax Building Society acquired Leeds Building Society and prepared to float on the stock exchange and become a fully fledged bank, Halifax and Leeds staff – burdened with huge workloads and stretching goals and deadlines – were immediately thrown together and were forced to resolve their differences as quickly as possible. Almost by accident, Halifax Bank emerged with an integrated workforce and a new culture that had successfully blended elements from the two former building societies.[7]

The four Cs

In a merger, people's commitment and involvement are too important to leave to chance. This book explores how companies can "engage" their people during a merger and find the best ways to link together their designed and emergent strategies and the integration process. The process of engagement has four dimensions.

- **Co-ordination:** informing employees about the combination so that they can see where they fit in.
- **Co-operation:** encouraging intellectual buy-in by creating opportunities for people to voice their thoughts and concerns.
- **Collaboration:** encouraging intellectual and emotional buy-in through creating opportunities to explore differences and similarities and appreciate complementary skills and experiences.
- **Commitment:** helping people to see that they have a stake in the business and moving them to a position where they want and know how to contribute towards its success.

Unifying essentials

This book argues that the integration process itself can be a powerful tool to ensure that the new business begins harnessing its intellectual assets from the very first day of the merger, and that companies that leave this task to be tackled at a later stage do so at their peril. A unifying theme is that every phase of a merger can be:

- built around the principle of employee engagement, helping to nurture an ever-widening sense of ownership and commitment to the new combination;
- tightly linked to the strategic vision and objectives of the combination and conducted in such a way that they help leverage the human capital within the combining organisations;
- managed in such a way as to encourage dialogue, upward

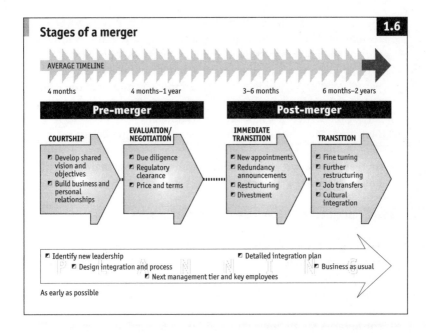

Stages of a merger

1.6

AVERAGE TIMELINE

| 4 months | 4 months–1 year | 3–6 months | 6 months–2 years |

Pre-merger | **Post-merger**

COURTSHIP
- Develop shared vision and objectives
- Build business and personal relationships

EVALUATION/ NEGOTIATION
- Due diligence
- Regulatory clearance
- Price and terms

IMMEDIATE TRANSITION
- New appointments
- Redundancy announcements
- Restructuring
- Divestment

TRANSITION
- Fine tuning
- Further restructuring
- Job transfers
- Cultural integration

- Identify new leadership
- Design integration and process
- Next management tier and key employees
- Detailed integration plan
- Business as usual

As early as possible

feedback and the flow of knowledge, ideas and fresh insights around the organisation;
- a source of personal and collective learning that can enhance the combination's capability and better equip it to handle future partnership arrangements.

Stage by stage

Further chapters examine the different stages of a merger. Pre-acquisition is characterised by the following phases (see Chart 1.6).

- **Courtship.** The respective management teams discuss the possibility of a merger and develop a shared vision and set of objectives. This can be achieved through a rapid series of meetings over a few weeks, or through several months of talks and informal meetings.
- **Evaluation and negotiation.** Once some form of understanding has been reached, the purchasing company conducts "due diligence", a detailed analysis of the "target" company's assets, liabilities and operations. This leads to a formal announcement of the merger and an intense round of negotiations, often involving

financial intermediaries. Permission is also sought from trade regulators. The new management team is agreed at this point, as well as the broad structure of the new business. This phase typically lasts three to four months, but it can take as long as a year if regulators decide to launch an investigation into the deal. "Closure" is a commonly used term to describe the point at which the legal transfer of ownership is completed.

◪ **Planning.** More and more companies use the time before completing a merger to assemble a senior team to oversee the merger integration and to begin planning the new management and operational structure.

Post-acquisition is characterised by the following phases.

◪ **The immediate transition.** This typically lasts three to six months and often involves intense activity. Employees receive information about whether and how the merger will affect their employment terms and conditions. Restructuring begins and may include site closures, redundancy announcements, divestment of subsidiaries (sometimes required by trade regulators), new appointments and job transfers. Communications and human-resources strategies are implemented. Various teams work on detailed plans for integration.

◪ **The transition period.** This lasts anywhere between six months and two years. The new organisational structure is in place, and the emphasis is now on fine-tuning the business and ensuring that the envisaged benefits of the merger are being realised. Companies often consider cultural integration at this point and may embark on a series of workshops exploring the values, philosophy and work styles of the merged business.

Chapter by chapter

Chapter titles reflect the metaphor that runs through the book of businesses as atoms, endlessly reacting and combining with each other through various tools such as mergers and acquisitions, joint ventures and strategic alliances. Mergers are likened to nuclear reactions that transform the core of the business, or nucleus, yet simultaneously unleash huge amounts of energy. This energy needs to be channelled to prevent it becoming a destructive force. The resulting "fallout" from a merger represents the stresses and strains of merging that can exact huge costs in human terms, causing great anxiety and stress among employees.

Chapter by chapter, the book breaks down as follows.

- **Fusion and fission:** examining the reasons why some companies successfully fuse together while others are damaged by the attempt.
- **Magnetic attraction:** looking at how management teams take the first steps towards committing themselves to a merger.
- **Analysing the atoms:** outlining various evaluation tools that enable companies to judge whether they should combine.
- **Creating a new nucleus:** arguing that integration teams can become the "positively charged" centre of the merged business and help shape its culture and personality.
- **Explosions and implosions:** looking at how the merger announcement, if handled badly, can send cataclysmic shocks through the combining organisations.
- **Minimising the fallout:** practical steps that managers can take to ensure that valued staff do not leave during the initial transition period.
- **Stirring the electrons:** surrounding the core of the business are countless "electrons" – managers who are responsible for the day-to-day running of the business. This chapter warns of the dangers of neglecting these people, as they can have a decisive influence on the ultimate success or failure of the merger.
- **Achieving fusion:** discussing how mergers can help release creative energy in the new business. This chapter was contributed by Michel Syrett, Visiting Fellow at Roffey Park Institute and co-author of *Successful Innovation.*[8]

2 Fusion and fission: M&A success and failure

MERGERS AND ACQUISITIONS help trigger change on a huge scale, often causing chain reactions within a business sector as companies combine in the race to gain competitive advantage. Like atomic reactions, M&AS release bursts of energy within companies, some of which are creative and some of which can be destructive. Some M&AS are successful in creating a stronger and more capable company. Others buckle under the stresses involved.

But first ... the "alternative M&A prospectus"

This chapter includes many reasons why companies choose mergers and acquisitions over other ways to grow their business. But these only go so far to explain why companies embark upon a course that has been shown repeatedly to have a difficult, disruptive and highly unpredictable outcome. M&AS are, at heart, human-based transactions driven by human impulses such as ambition and rivalry as much as by strategic good sense. Michael Porter, a strategy guru at Harvard Business School, puts his finger on the unique nature of M&AS when he declares:

> There is a tremendous allure to mergers and acquisitions. It's the big play, the dramatic gesture. With the stroke of a pen, you can add billions to size, get a front-page story and create excitement in the market.

What might an "alternative M&A prospectus" look like? Discussions with retired CEOs[1] have led Nick Krass of The Conference Board, a global business network and research organisation based in America, to suggest the following motives.

◪ **The quest for "bigness".** Many M&AS are driven by the simple urge to be bigger. John Johnstone, retired CEO of Olin, a producer of basic materials, complained: "We're swept up in bigness", and Peter Bijur, retired chairman of Texaco, an oil company, spoke of the importance of scale and size to today's global oil companies. Mr Krass explains:

*Two market forces – globalisation and a bull market –
arose simultaneously and became intertwined, creating a
snowball effect that has caused* CEOs *to become swept up
in bigness: bigger companies, bigger revenues and bigger
paychecks.*

◪ **Saving face.** Mr Krass boldly asserts: "Sometimes CEOs commit
themselves publicly to a certain goal, and if they can't make it by
means of growth, they will achieve it through acquisition". He
uses the example of Lawrence Bossidy, former CEO of
AlliedSignal. He says that as Mr Bossidy approached retirement,
he realised he would fail to fulfil his promise that the company's
revenue would grow to $20 billion by 2000. In order to save face,
Mr Krass claims, AlliedSignal acquired Honeywell in 1999,
boosting revenue to $24 million.

◪ **Short term pressure.** Alfred DeCrane, retired CEO of Texaco,
talked of the intense focus on quarterly earnings, thanks to the
availability of up-to-the-minute financial information supplied by
cable television and the Internet. He says:

*Analysts are constantly focusing on quarterly earnings,
yet they claim to have an interest in the long range, so
sometimes they are pretty schizophrenic.*

Other items on the list could include the following.

◪ **Boredom.** Nick Winkfield, president of Wirthlin Europe, a market
research firm, says:

*There comes a sense of "been there, done that", so after a
few years as a* CEO, *there's nothing else left to do but to
go for a big deal.*

◪ **Fear of being left on the shelf.** The sight of other rivals merrily
coupling exerts tremendous pressure on companies to themselves
acquire. James Crosby, CEO of Halifax bank, made little secret of
his preference for organic growth and his general belief that
M&As were more trouble than they were worth. After seeing
various banking mergers, including Lloyds with TSB, Midland
with Hongkong & Shanghai Bank and NatWest with Royal Bank
of Scotland, the bank finally gave way to pressure and made a
successful bid of $16m for the Bank of Scotland in May 2001.

◪ **Tit for tat.** Companies frequently mirror each other's
acquisitions. For example, Nestlé's acquisition of Ralston Purina,

an American pet-food manufacturer, has been mirrored in Mars's $1.2 billion acquisition of Royal Canin, a French pet-food manufacturer. BP's merger with Amoco led shortly to Mobil's merger with Exxon.

◪ **CEO "hubris".** Cary Cooper, BUPA professor of organisational psychology and health at Manchester School of Management and an expert in merger psychology, talked of ego-driven CEOs at a meeting at Management Centre Europe, pointing to individuals who favour M&As "for personal aggrandisement, usually because they aren't clever enough to grow the organisation organically". Research by Columbia University reveals that executive pride really does drive M&A activity (see below).

Anything you can do, I can do better...

Research by Columbia University reveals that executive pride is a reality. Professors Mathew Hayward and Donald Hambrick studied the performance of 106 takeovers (each valued at over $100m) between 1989 and 1992. They developed various indicators of CEO hubris, such as recent praise for the CEO in the media, and the acquiring company's performance just before the acquisition. The self-importance of the CEO was also measured by the size of his or her remuneration package compared with that of other members of the executive team.

The study revealed a correlation between CEO hubris and a failure to extract any value from the acquisition. The higher the level of hubris, the more likely it was that the acquiring company offered too high a premium for the target. This mistake directly damaged the acquiring company's shareholder value. The two academics concluded that CEO hubris causes executives to become overly confident about their ability to achieve better value from the acquired company.

The official story

M&As continue to be popular because of their ability swiftly to enlarge a company's pool of assets and resources. Like chains of DNA, companies combine their assets and capabilities to create something new – at least in theory. In industries undergoing rapid change, a merger or acquisition may be the only way for businesses to adapt and thrive. Strategic alliances, although often propelled by similar needs, do not give a firm's management the same control over assets or speed of response.

The strategic goals of M&As could be any of the following.

Economies of scale

In many sectors, size counts. Often involving second-league players, these types of deals enable companies to leapfrog their larger rivals and improve their revenues through various advantages based on size and scale.

In the oil industry, for example, the mergers between Exxon and Mobil and between BP and Amoco have turned them into what the industry calls "supermajors". Both merged companies are now competing head-on with Royal Dutch Shell. Oil companies are facing intense pressure to improve their competitiveness because of pressure on oil prices and increasingly expensive oil exploration. As a result of their mergers, the two new companies have been able to broaden their activities while lowering their cost structures.

Consolidation

This often occurs rapidly as industries regroup into a smaller number of big companies. For example, in the metal manufacturing sector, Canadian-based Alcan Aluminium merged with the Alusuisse Group during 2000 to form Alcan Inc, a $12.4 billion organisation employing 53,000 people in 37 countries. In the steel industry, Japanese companies NKK and Kawasaki have merged to create JFE Holdings, one of the world's largest steel makers. And another huge merger has taken place between Luxembourg's Arbed, France's Usinor and Spain's Aceralia.

A wave of consolidation is occurring in services sectors as well. In advertising, the three market leaders together spent $8.8 billion on major acquisitions during 2000 and 2001. Interpublic acquired True North, WPP acquired Young & Rubicam and Publicis acquired Snyder and Saatchi & Saatchi.

Media buyers are now consolidating. This is to help them fight back against newly formed media giants such as Vivendi Universal and AOL Time Warner, which are using their size to increase advertising rates. For example, Publicis, a French agency, has recently merged its media-buying business with that of Cordiant, a British rival.

Globalisation

Companies use mergers and acquisitions to achieve a balance between global advantages and local responsiveness. M&As also enable a company to rapidly achieve a global presence. For example, Kerry group, an

Irish milk processor and dairy co-operative, has used acquisitions to transform itself into a global player in the food and ingredients business. Its purchase of Beatreme, an American food ingredient company, in 1988 was a pivotal deal, opening up new markets around the world and setting the company on the acquisition trail.

Create or gain access to distribution channels
A lack of distribution has been constraining the growth of wine companies. According to Dealogic, a research agency, these companies, many of them family-owned businesses, are turning to large drinks groups such as Diageo and Allied Domecq as a way of solving the problem. By June 2001, 71 bids had been made for wine companies with almost $5 billion being offered. Foster's, an Australian brewing company, has been one of the most active acquirers, buying over $1.5 billion of wine assets in 2000 and 2001. In October 2000, for example, it bought Beringer Wine, an American wine maker.

Gain access to new products and technologies
Mergers between pharmaceutical companies are driven by the need to develop and launch blockbuster drugs that can individually generate $1 billion or more in annual revenue. According to McKinsey, a consultancy firm, 23 pharmaceutical companies merged during the 1990s to form the top ten players. The biggest deals were between Glaxo Wellcome and SmithKline Beecham (2000), Pfizer and Warner-Lambert (2000) and Astra AB and Zeneca (April 1999). Pharmaceutical companies are always on the lookout for ways to speed up their research and development process, which ranges from discovery, development and licensing to global launch and sales. Pooling resources also enables them to spread their risks and place a number of bets on emerging technologies, such as genomics and biotechnology.

Enhance or increase products and/or service
Large mergers between banks specialising in different sectors and between regionally based banks has led to a much smaller number of players capable of providing a full range of services, including investment banking, insurance, mortgage lending, retail banking and personal banking. For example, in July 2001, Allianz AG, a German insurer, acquired Dresdner Bank, the third largest bank in Germany. According to Dealogic, this creates the world's fourth biggest financial group, based on market capitalisation.

Increase market share or access to new markets

Car manufacturers have turned to M&As in this way. For example, the ill-fated deal between Daimler-Benz and Chrysler was done to broaden its market range. Ford acquired Jaguar, Volvo and Land Rover to develop a presence in differentiated segments of the industry.

Diversification

Diversification, once all the rage, went out of fashion in the 1990s as opinion switched to the view that companies should focus on their core activities or "stick to their knitting". However, a study of over 800 acquisitions by McKinsey reveals a group of American and British corporate acquirers that are surprisingly successful at growing through diversified acquisitions. Although these unrelated deals offered few opportunities for synergy, the acquiring companies profited from them because they managed the acquisitions so well.

Firms such as Thermo Electron, Sara Lee and Clayton, Dubilier & Rice were identified by McKinsey as having "grown dramatically and captured sustained returns of 18–35% per year by making non-synergistic acquisitions". Much of their success lay in applying a core competency to the acquired business. For example, Clayton, Dubilier & Rice was skilled at turnarounds. Sara Lee has used its skill in branding and retail to improve the performance of over 60 different acquisitions.

M&As in the "new economy"

The assets involved in the current generation of M&As are both physical and intellectual. They might, for example, include research and development capability, financial expertise, distribution networks, and manufacturing and production facilities. The creation of New Orange through France Telecom's acquisition of Orange demonstrates this combining of tangible and intangible assets. FT planned to use Orange's brand strength and marketing expertise to enhance its own mobile business. Orange's ability to offer its customers innovative services has been helped through its access to FT's R&D capabilities. The new company now has a much wider geographical reach and can offer better international services at lower cost.

Intangible assets lie at the heart of what is called the "new economy". Beloved by management gurus, the concept centres on the belief that the full market value of companies is derived as much (and sometimes more) from their intangible assets as from their tangible assets, or "bricks and mortar", such as production plants and expensive corporate sites. Among the valuable intangibles are the "intellectual capital" of a business, such as innovative ability, industry knowledge and managerial capability.

Work by Andersen, an international accounting and consulting firm, provides a useful interpretation of the logic underlying the large number of deals in the technology, media and communications sector,[2] which accounted for nearly half of all M&A global activity during 2000, although M&A activity in the sector has since slumped. The study reveals how companies have typically leveraged and recombined five distinct asset groups.

- Physical assets, such as land, buildings, equipment and inventory.
- Financial assets, including cash, receivables, debt, investments and equity. Many companies have used their financial assets, including stockmarket values, to make acquisitions and thereby acquire different assets.
- Customer assets, including various customer relationships and brands, as well as distribution channels.
- Employee assets, leveraged from a company's workforce, suppliers and alliance partners.
- Organisational assets, including leadership, strategy, organisational structure, values, brand, systems and processes, intellectual property, knowledge and innovative ability.

M&A strategies in the new economy

Andersen's study suggests that technology, media and communications companies are successfully using M&AS to achieve the following "value creation" strategies.

1 **Connecting** different assets to increase capabilities. For example, BSkyB's acquisition of Sports.com gives it online content and expertise. This complements its Sky Sports content and positions it well for the emerging broadband technology.
2 **Converting** existing assets to create new capabilities. The Andersen study points to Worldcom, which used its financial assets in the form of its stock value to acquire MCI, thereby gaining a considerable customer base.
3 **Blocking** rivals through acquiring assets that effectively block new market entrants. For example, Cisco's acquisitions typically enable it to gain access to

new technology that is still in the early stage of development. This enables the company to gain a firm grip on the associated expertise.

The new economy is perhaps simply a catchy phrase to describe something that everyone knew but did not formally articulate. A look at M&As involving "old-economy" companies reveals that their reasons for the deal invariably include both a better exploitation of physical assets and the purchase of intellectual capital.

Overall, the evidence suggests that M&As are strategies that enable companies to regroup their assets as and when the competitive landscape changes.

Defining M&A success and failure

According to *Investor's Chronicle*, "usually the first (and often only) reason chief executives who think they are worth their salt will give to justify a takeover is that it will enhance earnings".[3] The trouble is, the magazine points out, "even bad deals can enhance earnings" since profits from the acquired business need only to exceed interest payments to boost earnings.

So should the justification be that the deal will enhance shareholder value? If that is the prime aim, it is one that is achieved only in half of M&As. Quantitative evidence (detailed below) from deals made during the past decade show, unequivocally, that M&As fail to yield any significant gains in shareholder value. In many cases, the only beneficiaries are the shareholders of the acquired company. It is widely believed that approximately 50% of deals are successful judged by shareholder value, and that the remaining unions either contribute no value or actually damage value for at least the first three years of the combined business.

Glaxo SmithKline, a global pharmaceuticals firm, provides an illustration of how in the short term at least a merger adds little to shareholder value. Before the merger announcement in February 2000, Glaxo Wellcome had a market capitalisation of £66.2 billion ($92.7 billion) and SmithKline Beecham had a value of £47.6 billion ($66.6 billion). Even though there were good reasons for the merger, almost £20 billion ($28 billion) was wiped off the market value of the two companies. One year later, the value of the new business was £113 billion ($158.2 billion), constituting merely the sum of the two original companies.

Studies from around the world show that it is difficult to ensure that

M&As will generate any lasting financial value. They are notoriously difficult to manage. They disrupt business performance, often damage profits over the short term, distract the management and, ultimately, add little or nothing to the book value of the new business. Most of the time, the only people who can be confident of benefiting from the deal are the shareholders of the acquired business and a host of management consultants, lawyers and financial advisers.

Sane management teams would surely take to their heels when confronted by merger statistics such as the following.

- A Mercer Management Consulting global survey of large deals[4] reveals that only 37% of deals made in the mid-1980s worth $500 million or more outperformed their industry average in shareholder values in the following three years. The figure rises to a barely respectable 52% for similar-sized deals in the 1990s.
- A survey of 85 global acquisitions between 1997 and 1999 by PA Consulting and the University of Edinburgh Management School[5] reveals a 2% increase in average shareholder returns in the first 11 days after the announcement of the deal. In the next 100 days, this decreases to 8% below the industry norm. Surveyed companies gained no significant increase in shareholder value even when cost savings were the prime motive for doing the deal.
- Cambridge University's Judge Institute examined 77 large takeovers by British companies between 1990 and 1996. In the two years after the deal, shares in the acquiring companies under-performed by an average of 18%.
- Consultancy KPMG's 2001 global survey[6] reports that 70% of the combinations studied failed to add value.
- Large deals are more likely to fail. The Mercer Management survey reveals that only one-quarter of deals valued at more than 30% or more of the acquirer's annual revenue succeeded in outperforming their industry average.

The poor performance of M&As has provoked a steady stream of research for the past two decades. This concentrated initially on pre-acquisition issues, such as whether failure could be attributed to inflated prices or poor strategy. Although these factors are important, the conclusion of the majority of studies was that post-acquisition factors were a more critical determinant of success. More and more M&A studies reveal the importance of post-acquisition leadership, an effective integration process, and the need to gain the co-operation and commitment of employees.

For example, in a worldwide survey in 1998/99 by Watson Wyatt, a consulting firm, retention of talent (76%), communication (71%) and integration of cultures (67%) were rated as the three most critical activities in the integration plan.

The close connection between people and synergies is also revealed by research. For example, the Andersen research into the technology, media and communication (TMC) sector looked at common barriers to success. Respondents cited people-based problems, such as the length of time taken for management to adapt, a failure to integrate new technology because of a "not invented here" mentality, poor cultural integration and the failure to retain key people. The survey overwhelmingly pointed to the quality of leadership as the biggest potential barrier to successful integration. Respondents highlighted the lack of an executive champion (76%), an unclear strategy (74%), poor executive alignment (62%) and a failure to involve major stakeholders (61%) as the biggest potential barriers to success.

Post-acquisition problems can be grouped under the following three headings.

Poor performance

Many combining companies experience sharp dips in performance following a merger or acquisition. For example, Sema, an IT services group, acquired LHS, an American telecoms software provider, for £3 billion ($4.2 billion) in July 2000. By November, management was forced to announce there had been a "significant deterioration" in LHS's performance. Following the profits warning, Sema's market value plunged by 44% to £1.7 billion ($2.4 billion), causing its exit from the FTSE 100 index of leading UK listed companies.

The merger between Southern Pacific Railroad and Union Pacific Railroad in 1997 is another celebrated example. Following staffing problems and disruption to services, the merged company's earnings declined by 15% in the first quarter of 1997. After the first year, revenue dropped by $125 million.

The Watson Wyatt study confirms this typical dip in performance. It revealed a drop of 50% in the surveyed companies' productivity in the first five months of a merger or acquisition. A simple lack of concentration on the core business is often the cause – change-management specialists have a general rule of thumb that the productivity of employees falls to less than one-fifth of the normal average during any significant corporate transition.

Resistance to change

The reality of many M&As is that they are often extremely difficult and stressful events for many people. Merger studies reveal that employees need emotional support and practical skills in managing change in order to survive the upheaval. People can resist change by clinging to old behaviours and work practices, even when these are no longer appropriate. In rarer cases, individuals may actively resist change by being openly critical and hostile. This may even result in organised resistance through a trade union or a similar professional body.

At worst, employee resistance leads to people leaving the new business. Although it is difficult to quantify the scale of the problem, it is clear that many companies lose valuable staff in the months after a merger or acquisition. In some cases, people leave during the period between the M&A announcement and its legal completion (often called "closure") because they anticipate that they will lose their job or assume that the effects on their job and career will be adverse. Or they may stay for a few months to analyse their situation before "voting with their feet" and leaving.

There are few comprehensive studies of job losses attributable to mergers and acquisitions, but a number of international studies list M&As as one of a number of factors leading to large-scale reductions in labour in such sectors as banking, for example. Merger literature still cites an American study[7] conducted in 1986 of 150 large mergers and acquisitions as indicative of the true picture. This study reported turnover rates among senior executives of almost 50% within the first year of the changeover, rising to 75% by the end of three years.

Cultural "incompatibility"

Cultural friction is a difficult condition to analyse because it is "polysymptomatic", revealing itself in diverse problems such as poor productivity, wrangles among the top team, high turnover rates, delays in integration and an overall failure to realise the synergies of the deal. Much attention has been given to cultural issues and the need for companies to analyse their own cultural traits as a guide to selecting a combination partner and recognising and resolving cultural misunderstandings.

Cross-border deals must contend with the additional layer of differences in national cultures. A study of 319 European cross-border deals suggested a success rate of only 57%.[8]

Interviews with 142 senior executives of large European acquirers[9] suggest that the common problems inherent in acquisitions are compounded in cross-border deals by national cultures, language, politics and regulation. Some 61% of respondents believed that cross-border deals were more likely to fail. "Many suspected the 'foreigner's curse' – a target is for sale to a foreign company because local bidders know better," says Duncan Angwin, one of the researchers and a merger specialist at Warwick Business School in the UK.

A more rounded picture of success

If M&As are so prone to failure, why do management teams still carry on making deals? And do business people use the same yardsticks to measure their transactions as academics and consultants?

When Manchester School of Management interviewed 146 CEOs of the UK's top 500 companies,[10] the researchers found that the fundamental motive for acquiring was to maximise growth through improving profitability and market dominance. Against these objectives, over three-quarters of the CEOs stated that they viewed their company's acquisitions as successful. Some 63% said that this perceived success had influenced their decision to undertake further acquisitions.

The Conference Board discovered similar results when it asked 134 companies to judge their M&A success rate between 1990 and 2000. A surprising two-thirds of the survey participants reported a "very successful" or "successful outcome". Lawrence Schien, senior fellow of The Conference Board, comments:

> Given the negative view of mergers often presented by
> consultants, academics and the media, the fact that companies
> are reporting a willingness to cope with integration challenges
> is a positive, somewhat unexpected finding. Though spectacular
> M&A disasters receive a great deal of attention, companies are
> experiencing integration success with better financial results.

Andersen's survey of technology, media and communications companies also presents a positive picture of M&As. Some 77% of respondents reported their strategic objectives were "completely" achieved. When asked to evaluate the importance of various different drivers of M&A activity, 63% reported technology enhancement as very important;

98% said acquisition of talent was "somewhat" (58%) or "very" (40%) important. More than half of the respondents thought the acquisition of intellectual property was very important (51%).

Many of today's senior managers show a more positive and upbeat perception of merger success. Their comments plainly show that their perception of the success of M&As lies in their strategic value. In a lively debate about the value of M&As in the *Harvard Business Review*,[11] Alex Mandl, chairman and CEO of Internet services provider Teligent, declared:

> *I would take issue with the idea that most mergers end up being failures. When I look at many companies today ... I have a hard time dismissing the strategic power of M&AS.*

Mr Mandl pointed to his own experience of acquiring McCaw Cellular for AT&T in 1993. AT&T was criticised for paying too much for the company yet, with hindsight,

> *... it's clear that cellular telephony was a critical asset for the telecommunications business, and it would have been a tough proposition to build that business from scratch.*

Advertising giant WPP is another company that pursues the acquisition trail and that through acquisitions of firms such as Young & Rubicam now ranks among the top three advertising agencies in the world. WPP believes that most of its acquisitions are successful. It typically acquires small, niche players that have a proven track record in a range of advertising disciplines. Talent and creativity are important considerations, explains Laurence Mellman, WPP's director of special projects:

> *Culture is of fundamental importance in all our deals. The culture of a target business is usually the first thing that attracts our people. What they look for is talent, perhaps in the shape of creative people or very good account managers.*

The trouble is, it is difficult to measure creativity or knowledge and even harder to map their impact on the bottom line of any business. The M&A industry continues to concentrate on financial indicators because it is easier to do so and because it provides a useful sales context for M&A advice. The starting point of many of these studies is to refer to John Kitching, one of the first academic researchers to investigate the performance of acquiring companies. What they choose to ignore is Mr Kitching's warnings about the serious shortcomings of judging merger success on internal financial data such as return on investment, earnings growth and earnings per share. He argues that these figures are not always reliable for the following reasons.

- Data are often destroyed after an acquisition, making performance comparisons highly difficult.
- Numbers become distorted because of changes in accounting conventions, tax liabilities, transfer prices and head-office charges.
- Operational changes can become so substantial after a changeover that the company being measured no longer exists as a viable unit.

Mr Kitching concluded:

> A good measurement technique must recognise that management motives for making acquisitions differ and that the weight accorded to each motive differs. Thus ... perception of success or failure must be a composite measure setting current satisfaction levels against the original motives.[12]

Challenges of today's deals

This book follows Mr Kitching's advice by exploring many of today's deals in the context of their original motivation. From this starting point it follows that successful integration strategies must be linked to the overarching reasons for the deal. Integration approaches that help deliver the strategy can be judged successful and vice versa.

Today's deals are fuelled by the need to leverage both tangible and intangible, people-based assets. There is growing recognition that a company's intellectual and emotional assets constitute its distinctive capability. Companies that know how to leverage these capabilities gain a vital edge over their competitors. This process is difficult enough in ordinary times and becomes even more difficult during an M&A. But as more and more deals depend on achieving higher-level synergies for their success, arguably the most important challenge is to engage people during the integration process. The next chapter explores how the process of engagement must start from the moment merger discussions begin.

3 Magnetic attraction: initiating a merger or acquisition

MERGER TEXTBOOKS traditionally yield scant information about how M&A discussions get off the ground, other than to talk vaguely about the presence of "chemistry" between the combining companies. In reality, the initial discussions between the deal makers are like first dates, with each party gradually disclosing more about themselves as their relationship proceeds. Michael Mädel, president and CEO of advertising agency J. Walter Thompson (Europe, Middle East and Africa) comments:

> Part of a successful acquisition is spending time together. It doesn't mean you have to go on vacation together but you must take the time professionally over dinners to get to know each other. You need to feel there is someone on the other side with whom you really want to do business, that you are confident with and vice versa. There is no kind of formula in any M&A handbook for that process.

The courtship phase of an M&A is a brief window of opportunity where the people involved can make a decisive impact on the success of a deal. They have only a matter of weeks to judge whether they can do business together before accountants, tax advisers and lawyers are brought in to help negotiate and formalise the deal. An effective courtship helps minimise certain classic pre-deal mistakes, which were uncovered in a survey by Deloitte & Touche, a professional services firm, of 150 senior executives from *Fortune* 1000 companies.[1] When asked what was the major reason some M&As fail, the majority focused on pre-acquisition factors: 23% indicated they paid too high a price, another 23% said there was a lack of a compelling strategic rationale and the same percentage said there were unrealistic expectations of possible synergies.

However attractive the figures look on paper, the ultimate success of a deal depends on the ability of senior executives to be united about the strategic reasons for the deal and their vision of the potential rewards and benefits. Any suggestion of "blood on the carpet" or deep-running enmity between the two management teams will stop integration in its tracks. The loss of valued managers immediately after a deal is announced is also demoralising and shakes employees' faith in the deal. When Glaxo Welcome and SmithKline Beecham first started discussing a merger in 1998, they agreed the exchange of shares between the two firms, but talks ran into the ground over managerial roles. Sir Richard Sykes, Glaxo's chairman, clashed with Jan Leschley, SmithKline Beecham's CEO, about who would be executive chairman and CEO of the merged business. Neither side could agree on who should fill the other boardroom jobs and discussions broke down – a state of affairs of which the stockmarket took a dim view.

It is tempting to bury differences in order to conclude a successful deal, but they will only resurface during the integration process. For example, the different cultural approaches to negotiations of Daimler and Chrysler are now seen as the harbinger of the management conflict that so rapidly turned the deal sour. As one commentator said,[2] with the luxury of hindsight:

> The very different ways in which America and Germany handle international mergers hinted at future strife. The free-market approach to mergers in the US sat uneasily with the German protectionist attitude even before the contrasting management styles of Stuttgart and Detroit began to emerge as a bone of contention.

In another instance, managers of the Automobile Association (AA), a British breakdown and car insurance business, were so keen to link up with a bigger organisation to get a much needed injection of capital that, said a senior manager, they seemed "in violent agreement" with Centrica, a British energy distribution business, when it made a bid.

> They did not thrash out some important issues and some parts of the AA felt sold out by them afterwards. The AA's managers were so anxious to safeguard the organisation's future that they forgot to clarify their own positions. They were forced to fight for a place in the business after it was sold. People got very jittery and started to write CVs.

When firms are considering an M&A, they must:

◪ develop the case for an M&A;
◪ target a company and start "dating";

■ conduct an initial review of the target business's activities and competitive position, prior to formal due diligence;
■ explore potential synergies;
■ outline the broad parameters upon which negotiations will be based;
■ decide whether or not to propose "marriage".

These activities are not necessarily sequential. For example, confidential talks may be held with a small group of influential shareholders about their likelihood of supporting the deal at the same time as talks with the managers of the target firm are initiated. Negotiations are likely to run in parallel with a detailed analysis of the potential benefits of the deal. Due diligence, the process of investigating the facts about an M&A target, should ideally start early, so that as much relevant information has been gathered before media or other pressures to make some kind of merger or merger talks announcement become impossible to ignore.

The merger process is also shaped by whether the combining companies are private or public. When a private company is taken over, due diligence can be conducted alongside negotiations, culminating in a sale of purchase agreement. Once the merger or acquisition is announced, the transaction is usually completed rapidly.

When public companies merge, the process is often more complicated and more risky, especially in the case of a hostile takeover or a contested bid. One of the messiest in recent history was SunTrust Bank's unsolicited bid for Wachovia immediately after Wachovia had agreed a merger with First Union in April 2001. SunTrust had long tried to merge with Wachovia, almost succeeding in December 2000 before the latter backed out. Wachovia's board rejected the counter-bid, prompting SunTrust to sue Wachovia and First Union. SunTrust claimed the two companies had misrepresented the deal to their shareholders by overstating the value of the First Union bid. Wachovia retaliated by filing a suit against SunTrust for allegedly interfering with its business relationships. It accused SunTrust of misrepresenting information and unlawfully using confidential information in its bid, and it claimed that SunTrust broke its confidentiality contract with the bank by disclosing information gathered from due diligence carried out during its negotiations with Wachovia in December 2000. In the event, SunTrust lost its legal battle to block First Union. It also lost the battle to persuade Wachovia shareholders. Both Wachovia and First Union shareholders approved the merger, which was completed in August 2001.

Any potential bidder uncertain of the response to a bid may, shortly before making an offer (perhaps the day before), approach a small number of shareholders to see if they will support the bid. The British code on takeovers and mergers generally restricts the number that can be approached to no more than six shareholders. These may be persuaded to issue irrevocables, as Giles Money-Coutts, managing director of the M&A division of SG Hambros, an investment bank, explains:

> Traditionally, shareholders can agree to two kinds of irrevocables. "Hard" irrevocables are when the institutions agree that they will accept your offer and yours only. These undertakings are rarely given these days. "Soft" irrevocables are when the institutions agree to the bid in principle, but remain free to accept a higher bid if it is available. Irrevocables generally help shut out other bidders and your stance is that much stronger because the market is expecting the deal to proceed on a recommended basis.

According to Mr Money-Coutts, since the late 1990s there has been a trend towards shareholders issuing irrevocables that will be waived aside only if another company offers a material increase on the original bid, say 10% or more. When a firm rejects a bid, the bidder can launch a hostile bid by directly appealing to shareholders. In such circumstances, the due diligence process is likely to be restricted by the unwillingness of the target company to hand over any information.

Before launching a hostile bid, a bidder may seek to secure the support of a small number of key shareholders so that the bid is accompanied by a "bear hug". Mr Money-Coutts explains:

> The bidder tells them about the offer that has been put on the table and asks them to give them irrevocables so they can launch a bid with their backing. Alternatively, the bidder may ask these shareholders to talk to the target company and persuade them to enter negotiations. Normally, institutions don't like to put pressure on management, but bear hugs can become relevant tactics when they think management is failing to perform.

The early stages of a deal are typically handled by a small number of senior managers and strategists. Operational managers and specialists are drawn in at a slightly later stage to help formulate a detailed integration plan. Key players include a champion or sponsor responsible for overseeing the deal. Many companies advise that it is helpful for a senior manager who is not directly involved in the merger discussions to adopt the role of champion or sponsor. Ideally, this should be the chairman or someone with the standing and authority to act as an impartial "court of appeal" in helping to resolve disputes. The M&A champion also helps maintain momentum by keeping in close touch with the main players in the courtship and by ensuring that discussions stay focused on the big picture rather than on operational details.

A small group of directors typically constitute the core deal-making team. Until recently, human-resources (HR) directors were left out of this group, but there is evidence to suggest that their insights into the human dimension of mergers are increasingly being sought by their colleagues. In a survey of HR directors and managers from 80 firms by the UK-based Chartered Institute of Personnel and Development (CIPD),[3] 66% of respondents reported HR involvement during negotiations and a further 28% during implementation planning. Around one in four respondents considered certain HR issues, notably reward strategy, employment law and employee relations, as "critical to the viability of the deal or having changed the merger plans". However, when The Conference Board[4] interviewed 134 HR managers their clear view was that legal and financial experts have too much say on the viability of a merger and that HR managers, especially those in the acquired business, are not given enough opportunities to contribute to merger discussions.

"Matchmaker, make me a match"

Matchmakers come in all shapes and sizes. Companies that make a lot of acquisitions often have a dedicated merger team, perhaps based within corporate finance or corporate strategy. This team sifts through financial and marketing information in an attempt to match the company's pre-scribed acquisition strategy with potential targets. For example, CRH, an international building materials group based in Ireland, uses 14 development teams that operate globally looking for potential acquisitions and investment opportunities. The aim is to use acquisitions to build up leadership positions in local markets by either adding to existing activities or moving into new markets. CRH generally acquires small to medium-sized local businesses, often family owned (see below).

CRH: building a local presence through acquisitions

Acquisitions are an important part of CRH's strategy for growth. Harry Sheridan, CRH's finance director, estimates that since 1997 roughly 50% of CRH's growth has been achieved through acquisitions. During 2000, the company made five medium-sized deals at a total cost of €900,000 ($103,500) and 60 small deals totalling €700,000 ($805,000). The group made a further 22 acquisitions during 2001 at a total cost of around €1 billion ($1.15 billion). In CRH's terms, a successful acquisition earns a 15% return after three years.

CRH's strategy is to use an acquisition to establish a base in a new country. It then expands by acquiring local companies, usually retaining the management team. The group helps these businesses to build market leadership through expanding product lines, injecting new capital and providing technical and management expertise, particularly budget controls and reporting procedures.

Besides considering the target company's financial state, especially its cash flow and return on capital, the calibre of the management team and their ability to grow the business are crucial. The group's 14 business development teams keep close tabs on potential acquisitions. Mr Sheridan says:

> We talk to these companies over a period of time and build a relationship with them. We don't rely on intermediaries. We know these businesses are good because their managers are good and we want to keep them on board as we "bolt" their business onto ours.

Mr Sheridan strongly believes that post-acquisition problems can be minimised by frank discussions before the deal is done.

> Integration planning is not something that takes place after the deal is completed, it is part of the acquisition process. We talk to the acquisition's managers to try and find the right balance between maintaining their autonomy so that they can continue to respond to their local markets, while becoming part of an international business.

As well as retaining a stake in their business and receiving CRH shares, a powerful inducement for managers to join CRH is the support that they receive to grow their businesses. Managers can tap into CRH's expertise – group learning is encouraged through regular management meetings and a number of "best practice" teams are available to give technical advice. Mr Sheridan says:

> Having the resources of an international group is a great support for former small business owners. It gives them tremendous confidence to grow their businesses.

M&A strategy may be just one part of the corporate strategy team's responsibility or it might be given to a senior executive or member of the board. In international or global businesses, responsibility for finding suitable targets may be devolved to regional operating units because of their local or market knowledge. They might then have these decisions ratified by the group executive (see "M&A insights" below).

M&A INSIGHTS

Laurence Mellman, director of special projects, WPP, describes his role of co-ordinating M&A activity within the group

"The pipeline for our acquisitions is through WPP, as the parent company. We have a fairly limited role. Each main operating company is responsible for formulating its own global and regional strategy. They typically suggest a deal. My role, and that of my counterpart in New York, is to say yes or no. I provide advice about the strategic positioning of the potential target and the overall acquisition process. I might also advise about structuring and pricing a deal.

"When the decision has been made to make a transaction and the boxes have been ticked, I tend to step back and move on to the next deal. The operating companies take over the process of integration. As a parent company, we add value by providing strategic direction and by pushing our people to keep acquiring so we can reach our growth targets.

"We run a New Business Forum for the heads of acquired companies where we explain the way WPP operates, particularly its reporting structures and budgeting processes. During the forum, we discuss potential business opportunities. We introduce people to their counterparts in other WPP businesses and do everything we can to encourage networking. This helps us to continue our 'kiss and punch' approach whereby our agencies sometimes collaborate with each other to supply cross-marketing disciplines or compete against each other for new business, depending on what the client wants. This is a difficult balance to achieve, but we believe this is where WPP as a group contributes its greatest value. Inevitably, there are turf wars, but it is up to the centre to act as facilitator."

Gossip is often the spark that ignites an M&A. In many industries, the people at the top meet frequently and may have worked in the same companies earlier in their careers. Although it is impossible to calculate, large numbers of deals are initiated through informal conversations between CEOs in trains, planes and around dinner tables. When two CEOs are spotted at lunch together there is often press speculation about a merger. Two academics, Reingold and Barrett, argue that such cosy link-ups, where the parties "know each other and how they behave reputationally", are more prone to sloppiness. When the deal is being negotiated, they argue, there is too much reliance on trust and familiarity and not enough on objective analysis.

Intermediaries play an important role in matchmaking, but they should not be allowed to drive the relationship. Deloitte & Touche's 1996 study revealed that 89% of the surveyed companies were likely to use outside advisers during an M&A; of these, 45% said they were extremely likely. They used a variety of advisers: investment bankers (90%), lawyers (82%), accountants (60%) and tax advisers (53%). Charts 3.1 and 3.2 (on pages 44 and 45) list the top 20 advisers for announced worldwide and European deals during 2001.

Companies often commission intermediaries such as investment banks and management consultancies to identify potential targets and perhaps make initial contact before a formal approach is made. Conversely, a company might ask an intermediary to find a buyer, or perhaps arrange an auction. As Mr Money-Coutts says:

> Sometimes clients are looking for a key to unlock a situation – perhaps we know the management of the target business and we can act as a bridge, or perhaps we know something useful that will enable them to approach the deal in a particular way.

John Molner, a partner at Brown Brothers Harriman, a privately owned American bank, typically helps the owners of companies valued between $50m and $500m to sell their business. He comments:

> Before we start what is usually a limited auction, we approach a small number of potential buyers to see if they have an interest. Usually, our clients hire us to make senior-level contact with a prospective buyer, not just to send a fax. They want a relationship. They want to know they will be taken seriously before the formal auction process begins.

In other cases, a parent company may make overtures. However, the experiences of Homebase, the DIY subsidiary of J. Sainsbury, a leading

Chart 3.1 **M&A advisers, worldwide deals, 2001**[a]

Rank	Name of adviser	$ bn	Bids	2000 rank
1	Goldman, Sachs	667.18	344	2
2	Merrill Lynch	482.97	236	6
3	Morgan Stanley	461.31	295	1
4	Credit Suisse First Boston	444.27	405	3
5	JP Morgan	373.86	392	5
6	Salomon Smith Barney	252.60	325	4
7	Deutsche Bank	232.35	235	13
8	UBS Warburg	209.45	238	7
9	Lehman Brothers	133.66	154	10
10	NM Rothschild	125.40	177	9
11	Dresdner Kleinwort Wasserstein	123.35	99	11
12	Lazard	90.30	157	9
13	Bear Stearns	83.05	71	12
14	Quadrangle Group	71.95	1	–
15	CIBC World Markets	33.52	69	19
16	Greenhill	33.46	15	–
17	Bank of America	32.92	70	16
18	Cazenove	31.24	40	–
19	SG	30.75	91	–
20	Mediobanca SpA	30.10	25	–

a Excluding withdrawn deals and share buy-backs; including assumption of debt. Announced deals
January 1st–December 31st 2001.
Source: Dealogic

British supermarket group, strongly suggest that, in the case of an arranged marriage, the managers directly involved in the merger should still get to know each other. When Ladbrokes put Texas, its DIY business, up for sale, many Texas managers felt betrayed by their parent. Homebase bought Texas and expected its new staff to be positive about the deal because they would now belong to a major retailing group. Texas staff, especially managers and head-office employees, did not. Homebase found itself with the unexpected and unpalatable task of managing what was effectively a hostile takeover in the minds of many Texas people.

Potential targets could be any of the following.

Chart 3.2 **M&A advisers, European deals, 2001**

Rank	Name of adviser	$ bn	Bids	2000 rank
1	Goldman, Sachs	185.0	128	1
2	Morgan Stanley	149.1	124	2
3	Merrill Lynch	142.9	96	5
4	Credit Suisse First Boston	129.5	181	3
5	UBS Warburg	122.7	111	6
6	Dresdner Kleinwort Wasserstein	115.8	73	10
7	NM Rothschild	106.9	150	9
8	Deutsche Bank	106.7	131	12
9	JP Morgan	96.4	138	4
10	Salomon Smith Barney	90.2	132	8
11	Lazard	79.4	112	7
12	Lehman Brothers	47.4	57	11
13	Cazenove	31.0	35	15
14	Mediobanca	30.1	25	–
15	BNP Paribas	29.0	65	–
16	SG	24.5	56	–
17	Sal Oppenheim Jr	23.2	18	–
18	Greenhill	17.7	7	–
19	Gleacher	16.4	3	–
20	ABN AMRO	16.2	98	14

a Excluding withdrawn deals and share buy-backs; including assumption of debt. Target or bidder nationality is European. Announced deals January 1st–December 31st 2001.
Source: Dealogic

- Small, innovative start-up firms.
- Niche players that might have a useful capability, product or service.
- Smaller competitors, or promising "second-tier" businesses.
- Family-owned businesses which are either struggling or are experiencing succession problems.
- Divestments. A major acquisition or merger often involves a partner selling a part or parts of a business. Perhaps a decision has been made to sell non-core activities in order to refocus the new entity, or perhaps a regulator requires certain divestments to be made as a condition of approving the deal.

- Acquisition targets of competitors. If the deal does not go through there may be the opportunity to step in, or there may be scope for a counter-bid.
- Maturing joint ventures. The time is right to take full control, often because the JV has become more strategically important to one partner, or because the JV seems naturally to belong with one parent.
- Minority shareholding. The business has become more strategically important and the company wishes to take full control and ownership.

From dialogue to commitment

A positive foundation for the formal investigation and negotiation stage depends on establishing constructive dialogue. In the initial stages, people are inevitably wary, but it is important to work towards an atmosphere of candour. Ideally, both sides should be aiming to move through the stages shown in Chart 3.3. This is an iterative process, enabling the teams to move through each stage of negotiating a success-ful deal.

The process of moving from co-operation to collaboration and commit-ment must happen at every stage, starting from first contact, through to the signing of the deal and then, crucially, to the integration process, during which a range of challenges will need to be faced, some foreseen, some not.

Throughout the whole negotiating phase, it is important to:

- ensure the business case for the merger or acquisition is clear and compelling;
- create a constructive relationship at business and personal levels;
- get the support of significant shareholders and other important stakeholders.

A difficult challenge in the courtship stage is to build a relationship at what is often an exhausting and highly pressurised time. Because of the need for secrecy, the merger team is initially small, perhaps only three or four people. Mike Walsh, CEO (Europe, Middle East and Africa) of Ogilvy & Mather, an advertising agency that is part of the WPP group, argues that another reason for a small team is "the more confidential the process, the more both parties are able to share their innermost business secrets and ambitions".

The merger team has the prime responsibility for judging whether a

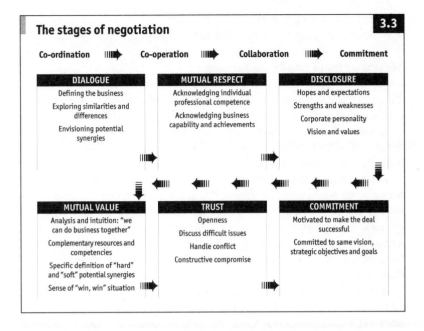

The stages of negotiation **3.3**

link-up is likely to succeed, on both commercial grounds and cultural compatibility. J. Walter Thompson's Mr Mädel provides the keynote for this chapter when he says:

> I cannot emphasise this too strongly – people sell to people. You cannot delegate it to lawyers or to financial people. The other company really want to see who is their partner. If there is a rapport developing, if there is mutual understanding and a feeling of trust and honesty, then you have laid a really strong foundation. If you don't have that, you will probably gain little from the acquisition.

The way early contact is handled between the two businesses helps set the tone for the rest of the transaction. "First encounters" speak volumes about how each party views the merger or acquisition. How managers speak and behave, and especially the language they use, usually makes it clear whether they view an M&A mainly as a legal transaction or a human-based event, representing a fusion of assets, intellectual capabilities and corporate cultures. Those involved in the merger talks need to ask themselves:

■ Are we making a deal or a relationship?

■ Are we paying more attention to the dowry than to the bride?

Mind your mind – and your language

It can be difficult to maintain a focus on the business relationship during the pre-announcement phase. Both sides must watch out for "merger mania". Many managers admit that the process of making a deal can be intoxicating. People get carried away by the excitement of the chase and make rash decisions – phrases like "shotgun marriages" or "marry in haste, repent at leisure" spring to mind.

Furthermore, much of the language used to describe and manage M&As is profoundly unhelpful for today's deals when the aim is, or should be, to build a relationship of trust and co-operation. Many phrases are adversarial (raids, white knights, poison pills, and so on), and other common terms, such as the "buyer", the new "owner" and the "acquired" company, emphasise the transactional aspect of M&As rather than their relational dimension.

Although it is common to talk of acquisitions or takeovers as mergers, this too can spell trouble. DaimlerChrysler has performed disastrously since the American and German "merger" in 1998, and it faces a lawsuit by Kirk Kerkorian, DaimlerChrysler's third largest shareholder. He claims that the deal was presented as a "merger of equals" rather than as a takeover of Chrysler by Daimler-Benz. He wants $8 billion in damages that in part is compensation for a takeover premium that he believes he would have received if the deal had been accurately portrayed. DaimlerChrysler is arguing that calling the deal a merger to its shareholders did not violate any securities laws.

Glaxo's "merger" with Wellcome also went sour, even though Glaxo adopted the term for the best of motives. Steve Sons, director of organisational effectiveness at Glaxo Wellcome Inc, an American subsidiary of Glaxo Wellcome, recalls:

> We started talking about this thing being a merger. It was probably better classified as an acquisition, but it was meant to be a friendly combination. The press took hold of it and started talking, causing employees from both companies to get upset. It became a hostile takeover in the eyes of the press and, once that happened, it became a hostile takeover in the eyes of the employees".[5]

Plainly, defining the M&A relationship accurately as well as sensitively is crucial.

Personal connections

It makes a big difference when the senior people involved make a special effort to establish mutual respect and understanding. For example, Bank of Ireland's purchase of the Bristol & West Building Society was greatly helped by a frank discussion of each company's hopes and expectations from the outset of the deal. Kevin Flanagan, one of the original four from Bristol & West involved in merger discussions with Bank of Ireland and now group human-resources director at BOI, explains:

> Our merchant bank had recommended that the two financial directors meet to discuss the figures. However, our CEO, John Burke, insisted that he should meet Patrick Molloy, BOI's CEO, to see if they could do business together. Burke felt strongly that whatever the commercial sense of the deal, the two organisations needed to feel they could work together.[6]

Both CEOs instinctively liked each other. Mr Flanagan says:

> They were very much on the same wavelength. Both were children of their organisations, working there for many years. They were strongly family men and, in their business lives, very concerned about hearts and minds.

Following the meeting between the two CEOs, each company chose a "gang of four" directors to meet over an informal dinner, steadfastly avoiding any talk of a possible link-up. Both parties felt they could work together successfully. By the time they entered detailed negotiations, B&W was ready to give up its much-prized independence and become part of a larger, international group. The negotiating teams were able to hold frank discussions about the "power dynamics" of the deal and the scope and limits of B&W's operational autonomy. Says Mr Flanagan:

> We accepted that the BOI was purchasing us and that if push came to shove, we would have to take a subordinate role. But Patrick Molloy was very sensitive and never pushed us into that position.

Negotiations between BOI and B&W succeeded because of an emphasis on creating a business relationship based on trust and rapport from the outset.

In partnerships, the process of putting together a deal is a different legal process, but the importance of building a shared commitment and understanding between parties is just the same. The merger between Price Waterhouse and Coopers & Lybrand required both firms' management teams to produce a prospectus and a document arguing the case for the merger prior to a secret ballot of each firm's partners. David Hadfield, the partner who headed PricewaterhouseCoopers's global integration team, says:

> Mergers between partnerships are difficult because you want to minimise uncertainty among your people by moving swiftly, yet you must work within a partnership structure that requires consultation. You cannot dictate what will happen. But in the event the vast majority of the partners gave their approval to the deal and this was a great endorsement for senior managers as they embarked upon what was a hugely complex merger, involving around 146,000 employees in 150 countries.

In any proposed M&A, the assumption must be that all the managers involved will identify closely with their own business and will be highly sensitive to any form of overt or covert criticism of its performance and track record. Mutual respect should be the cornerstone of any deal. From there, trust and openness can be built. As the relationship develops, difficult issues can be debated fully, resulting in a collective commitment to the overall M&A strategy.

In effect, those involved in the merger process must demonstrate the values and behaviours that they want in the new business. Ed Smith, responsible for global learning and education at PricewaterhouseCoopers, a professional services firm, says that the culture of the merged business will be strongly influenced by these early forms of collaboration. He comments:

> The job of leaders in a merger is to set the tone throughout the whole merger. They can send powerful messages about how the merger can result in a new combination of talent by working successfully with managers from the other business

*and by refusing to play safe by surrounding themselves with
their own people.*

This is crucial where the management teams of both firms will be
partly or wholly combined in the new business, or when the
owner/manager and senior managers of the target business will continue in their roles after the acquisition.

Developing the business case

This stage, in which the commercial logic for the M&A is developed, is a
curious blend of personal and organisational disclosure. Those involved
in the high-level discussions must not only give succinct descriptions of
how their businesses operate, but they must also describe the human
side in order to demonstrate the sense of the merger and the shape it
should take. Intuition and instinct play as important a role as analysis
and objective judgment. As Ogilvy & Mather's Mr Walsh says:

> *Intuition plays a big role. Intuitive judgment is key to deciding
> whether to make an acquisition. The "feel good" factor is not
> easy to describe, but if you don't feel good about a possible
> "marriage", you should stop the process.*

Thus the managers intimately involved in the merger process need to
be adept at recognising and solving business issues as well as those
stemming from personal or professional concerns. CRH's Mr Sheridan,
for example, emphasises the importance of understanding the personal
needs of the seller:

> *In a small company, cash isn't everything. An owner/manager,
> for example, may be very concerned about his personal
> standing in his local area. If he has built a local business and
> been strongly linked with it for over 20 years, it might be very
> important to him that we retain the name of the business.*

Mr Walsh agrees:

> *You must consider the emotional aspects of the selling party.
> Emotions can affect acquisitions either positively or negatively.
> During the selling process, the selling party will demonstrate
> emotional aspects, such as saying: "I am selling my freedom".*

*You must be sympathetic to their worries and arguments –
although the seller may have to give up certain things, both
parties must get the idea of a win-win situation.*

A number of common themes and issues dominate these early discussions. These can be grouped under the headings of strategy, performance, culture and organisation (see Chart 3.4).[7]

The priority given to these four areas varies according to the priorities
and mindsets of the different parties concerned. For example, Centrica,
the demerged distribution arm of British Gas (a former public-sector
monopoly), plainly placed much importance on strategy and performance during its negotiations to buy the AA. Off-the-record comments by
AA managers suggested that their bosses were more concerned about
finding a way to preserve the traditions and cultures of the AA, which
had been established in 1905 and liked to think of itself as "the UK's
fourth emergency service". These different priorities caused a lot of friction between AA and Centrica managers after the acquisition.

Perhaps the most important goal of these discussions is to ensure that
they are realistic and honest and that there are no surprises that might
derail the negotiating phase. Mr Molner of Brown Brothers Harriman
says:

*Sometimes teams try to market themselves too hard by
focusing exclusively on their competitive strengths. But any
potential problem or issue should be included in the first few
conversations, rather than in month two or three. In general,
we try to help teams present both issues and challenges and to
inform the other team at an appropriate time. If they don't,
they will find themselves revisiting the outline agreement or the
terms of the deal – which is always bad.*

Make the case compelling and clear

A clear message from successful M&As is that there must be a compelling strategic vision. In the words of Max Habeck, a principal at consulting firm A.T. Kearney in Germany:

*Without a bold "one-business" guiding vision, you may end up
with no more than numerous incompatible projects that can
dissipate the organisation's efforts and confuse its strategic
direction. In contrast, a one-business vision provides clear*

Chart 3.4 **Building a snapshot of the businesses: present and future**

Strategy	*Performance*	*Culture*	*Organisation*
current and future	*current and future*	*current and future*	*current and future*
◪ Strategic vision	◪ Financial goals	◪ Values and culture	◪ Structural design
◪ Business mission	◪ Strategic goals	◪ Identification of capabilities required for success	◪ Reporting structure
◪ Value proposition	◪ Key performance indicators		◪ Compensation
◪ Core competencies			◪ Shared services
			◪ Identification of capabilities for success

Is it compelling and exciting enough to justify a link-up?	**Will the numbers add up and increase the value of both organisations?**	**Can we really work together? Do we speak the same language?**	**Can we build something that is not just bigger but better?**

Personal issues	*Personal issues*	*Personal issues*	*Personal issues*
◪ Do they share my vision?	◪ Owner/manager: What will I be paid for the business?	◪ Do I want to subscribe to these values?	◪ Where will I fit in the organisational map?
◪ Do I have the strategic and leadership skills for operating in a different or broader context?	◪ What will be the interim payment structure if I stay on?	◪ Will my own managerial style fit?	◪ Who will I report to?
	◪ What will be my interim performance goals?		◪ How much autonomy and independence will I lose?
			◪ What power/status will I gain?
			◪ Personal remuneration?
			◪ Opportunities for professional development?

*guidelines for reconciling conflicts and reaching decisions in
the transition stage.*[8]

An example of an encompassing vision is AT&T's to become a "one-stop shop" for all telecommunications needs, encompassing fixed-line and cellular telephony, video and high-speed data.

In smaller acquisitions, the strategic vision may not be so panoramic, but it is nevertheless important. CRH's Mr Sheridan looks for management teams that will recognise the opportunity to perform on a bigger canvas:

> *The quality of the people that we take on is of paramount
> importance. We ask whether they have the ability to grow the
> business, with our help and support. Are they skilled? Do they
> have enthusiasm and vision? Do they share our vision?*

Both firms should be clear about how a link-up would help them achieve their objectives, perhaps by a radical route they would not have considered previously. They should translate (or define) the vision into a clear set of objectives and priorities and communicate this to all interested parties: shareholders, analysts, employees, suppliers, customers, and so on.

Strategic clarity is especially important when the M&A bandwagon is on the roll. Not only is it impossible for managers and other employees to identify potential synergies when they are unclear about the strategic logic of the deal, but the stockmarkets will be quick to punish the share price of companies that give no sign of knowing where they are going (see the Centrica and AA example, "Foggy logic").

Strategic vision is equally important when a firm has little M&A experience. As one manager said:

> *Sometimes, regional divisions may perceive certain
> acquisitions too tactically. It is important to avoid problems
> later on by getting these teams to make clear statements of
> their objectives and motivations.*

Intermediaries often play an important role here, as do M&A specialists in the parent company. (In this way, the courtship phase can also provide an opportunity to coach the target management team.)

Foggy logic

Centrica's £1.1 billion ($1.5 billion) acquisition of the AA in September 1999 was strongly criticised by business analysts, with some calling it "one deal too far". Centrica argued that the purchase was in line with its strategy to sell a wide range of goods and services with strong brand names to its customer base, one of the largest in the UK. It would gain synergies through sharing support functions such as call centres and billing. Centrica already sold gas and electricity, plumbing and air-conditioning services, and a range of financial services through its Goldfish credit card, home insurance and personal loans.

To many analysts, however, Centrica's purchase of the AA just seemed to confirm its status as "an old-style conglomerate", causing some to question whether the company's management were in danger of losing focus. Centrica's management had to put up with much scepticism and even derision, as one City commentary reveals:

> It is not obvious why putting boiler maintenance together with roadside rescue makes sense, even for such a frightfully modern company as the owner of the Goldfish credit card. There are no plans to train the gas fitters to peer under the bonnet at the side of the motorway (with the classic greeting: "Blimey guv, who put this in?") and do not expect the AA to offer central heating maintenance. Mind you, if gas-powered cars really take off …[9]

Off-the-record conversations with AA employees reveal that the strategic subtleties of the deal were equally lost on them. Ordinary employees found it difficult to accept Centrica's argument that the management capabilities necessary for running the AA were the same as those used by a former public-sector monopoly. The integration process did not proceed smoothly, and many of the AA's most experienced senior managers left in the early months of the changeover.

In relational terms, the task of discussing each other's respective strategies and competitive contexts can help forge a sense of mutual respect and understanding. Mr Sheridan comments:

> We obviously can't force people to sell their business to us. We usually have a good dialogue with them where we will tell them what we are about and how their business could help us

achieve our own goals. Our development teams will talk their language – they will have a good knowledge of the target management team's industry, and the day-to-day problems and challenges with which they are grappling.

Any merger or acquisition requires leadership commitment and energy. Ogilvy & Mather's Mr Walsh recommends:

You must excite the target company with your best work and your best people. Use the managers from other successful acquisitions to act as referees.

Those interviewed for this book acknowledged that they had several times made an acquisition to help improve the performance of a struggling division or subsidiary. One CEO said, for example: "We have used acquisitions to try and stimulate growth and profit performance in a subsidiary, or to inject better management expertise." However, his view reflects those of other interviewees when he says: "Our experience suggests that an acquisition is not an effective way to solve the problems of an existing business."

Numbers are number one
No company will embark on a M&A unless the numbers add up. As Mr Sheridan comments:

The strategy of an acquisition must be reflected in the numbers – the transaction has got to be worthwhile financially. We view the numbers as of extraordinary importance. We base our evaluations of an acquisition on its cash characteristics such as cash flow and return on capital. We have developed various financial multiples to help us form a view of the acquisition.

But as well as these financial imperatives, regular acquirers generally have a set of preferences unique to themselves, as can be seen by the characteristics sought by Ogilvy & Mather in the list opposite.

Target characteristics

Ogilvy & Mather places the highest priority on a target firm's client management, culture and climate. The managerial teams within the agencies making up the O&M group consider the following:

- professional excellence
- financial performance
- overall reputation
- stability of the business
- growth record
- aggressiveness
- attractiveness to clients
- client base (stemming from O&M's belief "you are the clients you serve")
- client retention
- creative or discipline reputation in the market
- management capabilities and reputation
- quality of employees
- chemistry with O&M

Cultural issues

It is obvious that corporate culture is crucial in any merger or acquisition that depends on collaboration for its success – which they increasingly do in the new economy. Surprisingly, the evidence is that although firms involved in the merger process may acknowledge the importance of culture, they rarely perceive it as a potential deal breaker. However, it seems to be the advisers rather than the "intermediaries" that take this view: of the 12 investment banks that were asked to comment on the human side of M&As for this book, only two people agreed to be interviewed.

Respondents in the CIPD survey (see page 40), who were human-resources managers, had a low opinion of financial advisers. One in five respondents reported that the financial advisers who helped in the process of acquiring a company had either a poor understanding of HR issues or none at all. When asked about the quality of advice that a target business receives, HR managers were even more negative. Nearly one in two respondents, or 46%, believed that financial advisers involved in selling a business had a poor or non-existent understanding of HR issues.

Culture must be discussed early on. More importantly, both sides should commit to including cultural auditing as a component of the due diligence process (see Chapter 4). This can help both businesses understand each other's cultures and gain a sense of the cultural traits that they hope to either preserve or jettison after the merger.

Even when human-resources people are used to facilitate discussions on cultural issues, all too often senior managers are uncomfortable with the process and what it reveals. In one international retail company, the director of organisational development had his offer to help turned down and culturally based disagreements soon emerged after the merger. It was only when three valued directors and several senior managers left the merged company in the first three months that it was decided that some team-building sessions would be a good idea.

There is also a tendency for managers to assume that a single, homogeneous culture exists throughout their organisation. In reality, many subcultures exist at the operating level, and some of these may well become major barriers to a successful combination. It is important that representatives from different parts of the company help identify potential areas of cultural conflict during the due diligence phase.

Cross-border deals have the added complexity of involving different national as well as corporate cultures. These differences often become apparent during negotiations, even among companies from neighbouring countries. For example, when MD Foods, Denmark's biggest dairy company, merged with Arla, one of Sweden's largest dairy firms, in 2000, cultural differences emerged immediately. Henrik Nygaard, product business unit controller for the new company, Arla Foods, says:

> The Danish and Swedish mentalities are very different. At the first couple of meetings, language was a problem. To us Danes, "yes" means "yes". To the Swedes, however, it means, "yes, let's think some more about it".[10]

Firms involved in a cross-border merger would be wise to consider using consultancies specialising in intercultural business in order to get to grips with the cultural issues involved and develop the managerial skills needed to deal with them.

At some stage in the courtship, the "cultural options" must be discussed. The four options are as follows.

- Cultural preservation: where the acquired company retains its cultural autonomy.
- Cultural assimilation: where the acquired company adopts the culture of its new owner.
- Cultural integration: where the two companies aim to take the "best of both" and create a new culture.
- Cultural transformation: born out of a melting pot of components of their own cultures as well as new practices and behaviours.

Which of these options makes most sense will, of course, depend on the type of business combination envisaged. For example, a small niche player acquired for its innovative ability will probably be given as much cultural autonomy as possible by its new parent. Although cultural insights will emerge during the due diligence process, it is helpful to start thinking seriously about cultural options as early as possible.

However, evidence suggests that although it is essential to analyse cultural issues, you must also realise that they are not easy to control. A major recommendation of one merger study is:

> Don't try to "paint the culture on" afterwards. The integration process itself, and how well or badly it is managed, helps mould the values and behaviour codes of the emerging organisation ... The so-called "soft" dimensions of culture, values, behaviours and working styles begin to take shape on the very first day of the merger.[11]

Organisational issues

In a straightforward takeover, organisational structure is often set in the mind of the acquiring company and there is little scope for negotiation. However, managers of the firm being acquired should be consulted and any concerns they raise should be examined to see if they have the potential to become significant problems, and whether some form of compromise, no matter how small, would be worthwhile. Not surprisingly, pay and benefits can be a sensitive area, and when there are significant differences in executive remuneration and terms and conditions, it can help to bring in remuneration specialists at an early stage to prevent the issue from stalling or souring negotiations.

The merger between law firms Clifford Chance (UK), Pünder (Germany) and Rogers & Wells (America) had to tackle the dramatic differences in the way partners were remunerated. Rogers & Wells paid their partners on the principle commonly known among American lawyers as "eat what you kill" – profits are shared out among partners based on how much business they personally win for their firms. Clifford Chance and Pünder followed the European approach of sharing profits among partners according to seniority, known as "lockstep". These different approaches had the potential to jeopardise the merger's goal of building a global law practice, where expertise and market knowledge would be shared between offices around the world. After intense discussions before the merger, the three firms agreed a compromise in the shape of a modified lockstep that enabled Rogers & Wells's highest paid partners to retain their earning system until sometime in 2002, when they would be paid on the same basis as other partners.

Allocation of the top jobs in the new firm is often highly controversial and can be the main reason for the failure of the M&A talks. For example, KLM and British Airways had the opportunity during 2000 to create the largest airline in Europe and the world's fourth biggest. However, merger talks were called off after three months of negotiations because of disputes over who would run the merged business.

To avoid such fallouts, it is often decided simply to merge the two management teams and then to allow "natural shrinkage" as managers retire. This was the solution favoured by Halifax and Leeds. David Jarrett, former head of succession planning and organisation development at Halifax and now retired, recalls that the new management team was accused of "fudging" the issue. He believes the decision was right, nonetheless:

> The single most important factor was to keep the show on the road. Yes, the team was a little unwieldy, but we believed the situation would correct itself over time as we redesigned our structures.

Jan Leschley, former CEO of SmithKline Beecham, shares Mr Jarrett's view and believes that an enlarged board is especially appropriate in mergers. "Board membership can be a very sensitive issue", he explains, no doubt speaking from his own painful experiences when his company's first round of discussions with Glaxo Wellcome were aborted in February 1998 because of disagreements about who should hold the top positions:

It is tough to face your board and tell half of them that they are not going to join the new board. It doesn't exactly create an easy atmosphere. Normally, you just combine the two boards as one big one and then over a year or two it comes down to a normal size again.[12]

Another controversial, even emotional, issue can be the location of the head office, because for many companies the corporate headquarters may be a potent symbol of its history, reputation and identity. A decision may be deferred, pending a detailed review of the businesses during due diligence, but it must be confronted and settled before the deal can be signed.

Merger negotiations between the Bank of Scotland and Halifax to create a £30 billion ($42 billion) business were reportedly delayed by the issue of whether the headquarters should be in Edinburgh, Scotland, or Halifax, England. According to the BBC's web newspaper:

Both Halifax, founded in 1853, and 306 year old Bank of Scotland are seen as business icons in their regions and closing either bank's headquarters would have been likely to provoke controversy.

BBC News claimed that the two banks made a trade-off. Instead of becoming the new CEO, as expected, Bank of Scotland's Peter Burt stepped aside and allowed Halifax to fill the two top positions in the merged group. BBC News reports:

Insiders insist he offered himself as part of a compromise, which puts Halifax chiefs in the driving seat, in return for Edinburgh claiming the corporate headquarters.[13]

Managers of the target company often have a different set of concerns that can make or break a deal.

Loss of independence

This is often a big concern when small firms are being acquired by larger ones, particularly when the small firm is led by an owner/manager. WPP's Mr Mellman talks about the need to reassure owner/managers about life within a much larger business. He explains:

WPP is seen as a tightly controlled business, dominated by a single individual, Martin Sorrell. Top people need lots of reassurance that they will be given considerable freedom and independence if they decide to sell their business to us. Very importantly, we communicate that they can run a piece of WPP's business. One of the best ways to reassure senior people is to get them in touch with other operating heads who have gone through the same experience – this approach usually works.

But owner/managers like the idea of being compensated by becoming bigger fish in a bigger pool. CRH emphasises the advantages of being able to benefit from the expertise and experience of a global business. Mr Sheridan says:

We let them know we have a set of standardised processes based on best practices that could help improve their business. We put the thoughts in their minds that we could help them get their productivity up and perhaps even increase their product range. Suddenly the thing becomes exciting to them. We are saying they can run something bigger and more successful.

For added measure, the company offers CRH options, "the glue linking the local situation with the group situation".

Loss of status

Some owner/managers may feel that becoming a "mere" manager is an unpalatable prospect, regardless of other business and personal benefits. J. Walter Thompson's Mr Mädel recommends wooing the individual by sending in the most senior person in the acquiring company.

As we are in a people business, the element of vanity plays a big role. We may know of someone who would be a great asset for the group but who really cannot see themselves reporting to a local country manager. We will not let an opportunity go just because of that issue, so I approach them directly.

Money

Owner/managers often have unrealistic expectations about the amount of money they will receive when they sell their business. It is common for them to receive a large sum when the deal is done, then a series of payouts over the next five years or so, depending on whether the business achieves a set of agreed performance targets. Such "lock-in" arrangements are used when the value of the business and its continuing success are perceived to depend on retaining some or all of the previous management. Because of their emotional closeness to their business, it can be sensible for owner/managers to employ advisers to negotiate the terms of the deal.

Making a decision

When it is decided to go ahead with an M&A, a sale of purchase agreement is issued if the acquisition is of a privately owned company. If the acquisition involves a public company, the markets are informed through a "letter of intent". This statement, which is subject to shareholder approval, typically outlines:

- the objective of the merger or acquisition;
- the financial and operational implications of the deal;
- assumption of debt requirements;
- the relevant assets and business units included in the transaction;
- the equity composition of the respective companies;
- various transactional details pertaining to liabilities, tax matters and indemnities.

By this stage the teams should have:

- developed a forceful and attractive strategic vision;
- identified a range of potential synergies as part of the business case;
- developed a rapport and a reasonable degree of openness and trust;
- performed a preliminary analysis of how the two businesses will fit together;
- explored personal and organisational issues and concerns that might derail formal negotiations.

If both teams are not wholeheartedly prepared to commit to the deal by the end of this process, they should think seriously about abandoning it. As the following chapters will show, the task of integrating two different organisations is highly complex and demanding. If they are to demonstrate effective and unified leadership, both parties must be equally committed to the success of the deal.

A decision to seek a merger must take into account strategic, financial, cultural, organisational and personal factors, according to the relative weight each factor is given. Objective analysis is critical – it can become difficult to walk away from a deal in which a lot of time and energy has been invested, especially if investors and analysts are hoping for something to happen.

Through examining 40 acquisitions, London Business School (LBS) has generated a useful list of ways managers can improve the likelihood of a merger succeeding. To a large extent, they are simply facets of good behaviour and common sense – all the more important as M&A courtships can sometimes bring out the worst behaviour. The LBS list includes the following.[14]

- **"Ordered interfaces".** In 77% of the successful acquisitions studied, leaders created ordered interfaces, deciding quickly which parts of the business should be kept or sold off, what would be managed by whom, and the degree of autonomy that would be allowed.
- **Clear vision.** In 68% of successful acquisitions, leaders demonstrated a clear vision about the future. This helped minimise uncertainty and kept everyone focused on business issues.
- **Persuasiveness.** In 64% of successful deals, executives in the acquiring company convinced executives in the target company that there were clear benefits to the deal.
- **"Honourable rhetoric".** 59% of successful management teams stuck to their promises and assurances.
- **"People-shaped" decisions.** 59% of successful management teams demonstrated their concern for people by making people-shaped decisions, rather than taking a theoretical or mechanistic approach.

The following chapter examines the next stage of a merger when due diligence is conducted, which helps to audit a company's assets and competitive position.

4 Analysing the atoms: building a picture of the merger partner

THE PREVIOUS CHAPTER examined the process of establishing a successful courtship and highlighted the range of professional and personal issues that must be resolved as early as possible. But hand-in-hand with the relational process of making a deal is the evaluation process, where all kinds of financial, marketing and cultural information are gathered and analysed in order to confirm:

◾ the correctness of the overarching M&A strategy;
◾ the judgment that the organisations are compatible, in terms of both business aspirations and corporate culture and personality.

Typically, the evaluation process is closely linked to the due diligence process, where various components of a company are rigorously audited. Due diligence should be the bridge between the pre-acquisition and post-acquisition phases. It should provide enough information to help reach a reasonable evaluation of the business to be acquired or merged with. The information should be fed into negotiations and help flesh out the terms of the deal. Lastly, the results of due diligence should be fed into the integration plan, especially where it relates to potential synergies, or when there are problems that must be tackled once the deal is closed. During this period, the combining companies should notify trade regulators (such as the Securities and Exchange Commission in America and the Merger Task Force in the EU) of their intentions. If a full-scale investigation is launched, the completion of the deal may be delayed by several months.

The disastrous link-up between Daimler-Benz and Chrysler is now attributed as much to a failure of due diligence as to hubris. The process apparently did not reveal serious flaws in Chrysler's product lines and overall competitive position: its minivans were ageing and their successors made little impact in a saturated market; Japanese and European competitors were squeezing its hitherto fat margins on vehicle sales; the cost of technical development was rising rapidly; and environmental regulations were becoming more onerous and costly. The cultural differences between the American and German firms appears to have received only a "nod and a wink". All the signs were that Chrysler would not be able to maintain its leading performance, yet still Daimler-Benz enthusiastically courted its transatlantic bride.

The *Economist's* interpretation[1] was that the egos of executives undermined the due diligence process:

> Acquisitive companies such as Daimler-Benz spend millions of dollars on "due diligence". But there is always pressure for the financial and legal diggers to come up with answers that vindicate the hunches of bosses who dreamt up the deal in the first place. Bosses, for their part, may be falsely reassured by the due diligence process, unaware that they are often hearing the echo of their own thoughts.

The point of due diligence is to help you keep your feet on the ground and to see your prospective partner for what it really is. But it is important that intuition, imagination and a spirit of collaboration are not stifled by the sheer weight of work that the due diligence process requires. Strategic vision, flair and energy can be lost in the maelstrom of detail that will hit the merger team. Numbers of all kinds will threaten to take over, as advisers and experts produce volumes of figures, graphs, ratios, metrics, financial models, and so on. Added to this is the possibility of negotiations stalling, perhaps for months, because of some kind of technical or legal difficulty. The excitement that was so painstakingly built up during the initial courtship can be dissipated if the merger team does not supply strong leadership and retain a tenacious grip on the original vision and goals.

The role of visionary must now be coupled with that of strategic sponsor. The evaluation phase marks a decisive shift in the courtship phase. Discussions are no longer private and informal. The small core of managers who initiated discussions must now begin to draw in other players, such as functional specialists. The teams may decide to employ a small team of strategy consultants to help them develop their merger plan. With the exception of large corporations, which often have their own specialist staff to work on deals, external specialists, such as lawyers, accountants, tax experts and business analysts, will help gather information and negotiate the deal. Due diligence teams made up of internal staff and external specialists must be formed, each with its own areas of responsibility.

Managers on the merger team must now operate in a more public arena, interacting with a variety of interested parties while keeping the proposed merger on track. As strategic sponsors, they must strive to ensure that everyone understands the vision and commercial case for the link-up, while also balancing the needs of the different groups involved.

The evaluation process should not be seen as a stand-alone process – something that is done by experts, often external consultants, for the purpose of negotiating the best price, terms and conditions. In today's deals, when the value of a business stems as much from its intellectual capital as from its physical assets, the task of business evaluation needs to be tightly linked to the strategic rationale for the deal and to the wider issue of cultural compatibility between the two firms. Just as important as financial and legal considerations are a company's unique capabilities, cultural strengths and weaknesses, managerial style and depth of leadership.

How the analysis is conducted is also important. Due diligence teams must probe widely and deeply, but they must take care not to harm the developing business relationship by being arrogant, dismissive or overly secretive. They are in effect ambassadors or harbingers, sent out before the main party arrives – should they upset the bride, the bride-groom is hardly likely to be welcomed.

In order to fulfil this function, they must be briefed on the nuances of the deal, the emotional tempo of the courtship and any controversial or contentious issues that they might inadvertently stumble upon.

Due diligence teams also need to recognise that their presence in a target organisation is likely to generate rumours and anxiety among employees – even when the M&A is unlikely to cause any redundancies. For example, the store manager of a retail outlet reacted to the purchaser's due diligence team as follows:

> We had lots of "grey suits" looking around. We knew we were being eyeballed, that they were peering at us, but nobody said anything or gave us any feedback.

The store manager and his team viewed the due diligence teams as "hatchet men", looking for any opportunity to "slash and burn". Such a reaction is common among employees who have not been informed that a merger or sale is under consideration. Members of the due diligence team may see themselves as objective auditors, but employees are often quick to suspect that they are making all kinds of value judgments about how the business is run. Employees can become prickly and defensive if mishandled by those carrying out due diligence, which will result in a less rich and comprehensive profile of the business.

Employee consultation and relationships with trade unions and works councils are often crucial to the success of an M&A. Not only does it make sense to get everyone on side, but regulations must often be complied with. In the EU, the Transfer of Undertakings (Protection of Employment) Regulations 1981 (TUPE)[2] apply to acquisitions that involve the transfer of a business, or part of a business, to another company. They do not apply to acquisitions that simply involve a share purchase. (M&As that involve organisations with employees in more than one EU member state may also need to take account of the Trans-National Information and Consultation of Employees Regulations 1999.) In the case of a transfer of business, TUPE requires that employees transfer automatically on their existing terms and conditions, including collective bargaining agreements. Changes in terms and conditions after the acquisition, for example to harmonise them with other parts of the business, may be invalid under TUPE regulations, which also stipulate when and how companies should inform and consult employees (see below).

TUPE: talking to employees before the deal is done

Companies must now follow a new set of obligations about informing and consulting employees. In theory, consultation should take place not once the deal is done, but when a company begins to contemplate a potential transfer of all or part of its business. (Different timescales may apply if redundancies are involved.) The company must tell employees that a transfer is likely to happen and what it is likely to mean for them. Employees should be given the opportunity to express their views, although they cannot block a transfer. They must convey their views via an employee representative.

Under the amended TUPE, employee representatives must include the appropriate trade union representatives if the company recognises an independent trade union. If no union exists:

- employees can choose existing employee representatives, for example, members of staff forums or works councils;
- affected employees can elect their representatives, using a process stipulated by TUPE.

If employees fail to elect representatives, their employer is still required to inform each affected individual of the proposed changes.

Companies have long argued that they should not be forced to divulge highly sensitive commercial information, especially before a deal is formally agreed, but the amended TUPE firmly safeguards employment rights. Under the regulations, companies that fail to inform and consult with employees are required to give up to 13 weeks actual pay per affected employee (that is, those who are affected by the merger and whose rights are altered). One potential loophole, the argument that a parent company organised the sale or transfer of a subsidiary without it knowing, is no longer accepted as a defence.

Determining the scope of due diligence

Due diligence lasts anywhere between five to 16 weeks, according to a survey of mergers and acquisitions by Watson Wyatt, a consulting firm.[3] There are several components of due diligence.

- ◪ Financial
  - · financial performance to date
  - · the balance sheet and profit and loss
  - · demand and capacity projections
  - · potential economies of scale
- ◪ Commercial
  - · size and growth
  - · lifestyle stage
  - · product mix
  - · pricing
  - · distribution channel mix
  - · route to market
  - · customer base
  - · current and future competitive position
- ◪ Human resources, typically focusing on the financial aspects, such as:
  - · compensation and benefit plans
  - · pension provisions
  - · severance
  - · employment contracts, especially clauses regarding a takeover
  - · any form of liability, such as pending employee relations lawsuits or trade union action

- cultural analysis, such as values, management style and customer care philosophy
- Managerial and organisational, including:
  - structures, processes and systems
  - strengths and weaknesses of the management team
  - nature and degree of difference between the combining organisations
- Technological, looking at:
  - production and information systems (these are increasingly regarded as critical in mergers because of the difficulty that companies often experience when trying to integrate their information systems)

In an ideal world, due diligence would be carried out in all these areas – and would be carried out with equal diligence by a firm looking for a buyer as well as vice versa. In reality, the scope and depth of due diligence are determined by the timing of the deal and antitrust regulations that set certain limits on the level of disclosure allowed before a merger or acquisition. Another important factor is whether the companies concerned are public or private. Public companies generally hold large amounts of quantified information and data about their operations. However, because a public company is obliged to allow all bidders access to the same information, it may be less willing to disclose information, even to a desired bidder. Private companies may be more willing to disclose information, but the data may be less sophisticated or less reliable.

Due diligence can be said to provide the evidential underwriting for any M&A, yet as John Ormerod, managing partner of Andersen UK, an accounting and consulting firm, explains:

> Too many transactions are rushed through before due
> diligence has been completed and robust plans are in place to
> carry the process through. While the acquirer may be forced to
> adopt a timetable set by the vendor and its advisers, or by
> market regulatory requirements, operational due diligence
> must still be a top priority.

Denzil Rankine, CEO of AMR, a London-based research consultancy specialising in commercial due diligence, agrees:

*Until the 1990s, acquirers devoted disproportionately limited
resources to understanding the markets into which they were
buying and to analysing an acquisition candidate's position
within them. They looked at the numbers and trusted the views
of management. Then in 1989, at the close of the 1980s
acquisition boom, Ferranti bankrupted itself when it acquired
ISC without having investigated the company's customer base;
this marked a turning point in acquisition thinking. A rigorous
approach to commercial due diligence helps acquirers to
negotiate better, reduce risk and avoid disaster.*

Watson Wyatt's 1998/99 M&A survey provides a useful list of the
information that companies gather during due diligence (see Chart 4.1
on the next page). The information most sought related to the value of
tangible assets and market share, and the report highlighted the incon-
sistency surrounding cultural issues:

*Cultural compatibility was consistently rated as the biggest
barrier to successful integration, yet results indicate this area is
the least likely to be researched during the due diligence phase.*

Another striking disparity is that only 49% of companies examined
"workforce potential", yet 76% said that the retention of talent was of
critical importance during the integration phase. How can companies
retain talented people during integration when they have failed to conduct any kind of audit of that talent?

One possible interpretation of these results is that human-resources
managers did not have sufficient input into the design of the due diligence process. Another is that some of the surveyed companies conducted due diligence without the knowledge or co-operation of a target
company. Such secrecy is sometimes necessary, but it must make a true
merger of minds and hearts more difficult if not impossible to achieve.
Successful mergers depend on building a shared vision of the future.
The creation of higher-level synergies over the longer term requires
deep collaboration across many different functions and levels. Due diligence should contribute towards this collaboration, not undermine it.

Managing due diligence

Responsibility for the due diligence process must be given to a senior
manager with strong strategic skills, commercial awareness and financial

Chart 4.1 **Information gathered through due diligence**

Information	%
Tangible assets	90
Market share, distribution	86
Technological and business competencies	78
Financial aspects of human-resources function (ie pensions and benefits)	75
Management capabilities	71
Major shareholders	56
Human-resources policy matters (ie labour relations, employment contracts)	56
Workforce potential	49
Organisational culture	46

Source: *Watson Wyatt's Worldwide 1998/99 Mergers and Acquisitions Survey*, 1999

expertise, and the ability to understand the organisational and cultural issues upon which success will depend. In deciding what factors are most critical to making a success of the merger, the following should be taken into account.

- The envisaged synergies – whether based primarily on physical, financial or intellectual assets.
- The M&A philosophy – based on various preferences such as the stage of a target company (ie, young start-up or mature business) cultural make-up (similar/complementary/different) and management style.
- The proposed degree of integration – for example, remaining independent, or linking together certain parts of the business such as IT and procurement, or a complete merger.

The due diligence process should focus on the M&A's sources of potential synergy, or strategic leverage, and the critical success factors. For example, if the success of the M&A rests on successfully sharing and leveraging technical skills, one critical success factor is to retain this expertise. The due diligence process should accordingly identify the individuals and groups that have the crucial skills, and also the operational or cultural infrastructure that enables the technical expertise to be harnessed effectively. Furthermore, the process needs to discover whether any golden parachutes or "accelerated vesting" may be triggered as a result of the company's sale, thereby giving valued individuals a financial incentive to leave.

Ideally, there should be no more than six critical success factors, which should be equally weighted between short-term synergies that can be achieved easily once the deal is signed, and longer-term synergies. In a comprehensive and valuable guide to commercial due diligence,[4] Mr Rankine also advises of the need to be guided by critical success factors that enable the target company to be successful in its specific market. He emphasises the need to keep reviewing the overarching objectives set out at the outset of the process:

> *Every effort must be made to define the correct information objectives when a commercial due diligence programme is launched ... It is equally important that the information objectives are reviewed as the work proceeds. As the picture of the company, its management and its market emerges, those issues that were considered important at first often melt away as new issues critical to the success of the business become clear.*

Any form of due diligence draws on the following sources.

- Information already in the public domain, for example, trade directories, newspaper articles, buyers' guides, brokers' reports and commercial databases.
- Fresh research based on, for example, discussions with customers, suppliers, distributors, alliance partners, former employees, competitors, business journalists, analysts and industry experts.
- The target company, through its management accounts, interviews with managers at various levels and internal data on, for example, customer satisfaction and employee turnover.

Leadership and firm guidance is critical in due diligence. Team leaders with strong project management and communications skills should be appointed to:

- oversee progress;
- ensure controls are in place to guarantee confidentiality;
- identify issues that the merger team need to understand;
- keep the team focused on the bigger picture;

■ adjust objectives and the scope of the process as it proves necessary;
■ liaise with other due diligence teams.

Selecting team leaders

Due diligence can be carried out by internal staff or external consultants, or a combination of both. A company may hire specialist help because it lacks the relevant expertise or sufficient internal resources, or because it does not want to fuel rumours of its interest in the target business. In rarer cases, using external consultants may help persuade sceptical directors of the merits of a link-up.

Mr Rankine believes that external consultants have a valuable role to play because of their objectivity. He explains:

> Acquisitions can consume considerable amounts of managers' time. This often creates an onus for success as managers fear that colleagues may challenge their judgment for spending many months on a deal that does not lead to fruition.

A further reason, he contends, is that:

> [A proposed deal] can change the shape and direction of companies. In any deal champions can, quite rightly, emerge for causes. Emotions can take over. In these circumstances, the objectivity of outsiders such as non-executive directors and consultants is essential.

Tatyana May, general counsel and company secretary at Shire Pharmaceuticals, formerly worked for Zeneca (now AstraZeneca) and helped sell its agrochemicals division to Novartis. She strongly believes that whether staffed by internal or external people, the team should ultimately be lead by managers from the client company.

> No matter what, investment bankers will have their own agendas. As project manager, my allegiance is to my company. I analyse any deal, not just on a strict legal basis but according to the needs of the business. Unlike an external consultant, an internal project leader has an awareness of how certain issues could impact the business, how the business is likely to respond and who needs to be informed internally. Their

> *perceptions are influenced by their sense of the history and context behind a business area or issue and they have a pretty good sense of where the different work-streams are and how they see things. Their strategic understanding helps them focus on what the business really wants out of the deal.*

Whatever the composition of the team, members should have a sound knowledge of the sector concerned, a solid track record in conducting due diligence and an appropriate mix of experience so that they will recognise the full commercial implications of whatever they discover about the target business.

It is also important that the due diligence teams regularly meet the senior person championing the merger to share their findings and discuss the implications for the integration plan. Indeed, in any acquisition made by GE Capital, the financial services arm of GE, a diversified services, technology and manufacturing company, the head of the due diligence process holds a series of daily meetings with the leaders of the different due diligence teams (typically finance, operations, systems, human resources and sales) to discuss what they had learnt each day.

Human capital due diligence

Human capital due diligence stems from the recognition that a company is made up of a rich blend of capabilities, cultures, values and philosophies that help determine its distinctive personality, which in turn influences its brands and the way it delivers products and services to its customers. Kevin Thomson, author of *Emotional Capital*,[5] is zealous about the importance of harnessing the commercial power of the corporate personality. He comments:

> *In reality, the only differentiation point, the final USP (unique selling point), the only sustainable advantage is an organisation's personality. It shines through in everything that is said and done ... Everything else about your business can be replicated: your product, your service, your added value.*

In Mr Thomson's terms, corporate personality consists of intellectual capital – information, knowledge and expertise – and emotional capital, "the hidden resources of feelings, belief, perceptions and values".

Human capital due diligence is a new offshoot of traditional due diligence and has several elements.

Intellectual capital

Every company has important pools of knowledge, some codified in the form of manuals, internal websites or dedicated best practice teams, some "tacit", meaning that it remains in the heads of skilled employees. Clifford Chance, for example, has codified knowledge in the form of standard form templates and examples of how these have been used. It also has an internal database, which can help on best practice, and has launched several online services, used by both employees and clients, which provide regularly updated advice on areas such as data protection regulation, cross-border financing and international sanctions.

Since its merger with law firms in Germany and America, Clifford Chance has worked hard to define the tacit knowledge that will help it achieve its ambition to become a global law firm. A principal goal of the merger is to ensure that staff around the world share their experience and understanding of their local context. The firm's managers view knowledge management as an important part of their role. Jim Benedict, head of Clifford Chance's litigation and dispute resolution practice, comments:

> *Certain parts of the litigation practice are global and others are more locally focused. Part of my job is learning what others do, taking the best from what they do and applying it elsewhere within the global practice. You look to people who are successful and try to support and build on their success.*

Clifford Chance managers believe that company culture is inextricably linked to intellectual capital. Paul Greenwood, the firm's newly appointed director of knowledge and information, asserts:

> *The key to successful knowledge management is culture. It's important to have a culture where everyone is inspired and has the freedom to think innovatively and creatively. Our merger has helped generate a sense of excitement – the feeling that anything is possible.*

The due diligence process should uncover some aspects of a company's intellectual capital, but, as yet, has rarely been linked to the kind of analysis that will help uncover the cultural infrastructure that supports more intangible sources of intellectual capital such as learning, knowledge sharing and innovation. These days, however, intellectual capital is becoming easier to audit. A growing number of knowledge-intensive businesses, such as legal firms, consultancies and financial-services providers, are aware of the value of their intellectual assets. For example, Allan Frank, chief technology officer at KPMG, once described the consultancy as "basically a giant brain. For us, the knowledge management environment is the core system to achieve competitive advantage". Many of these companies are making serious efforts to calculate their intellectual assets. For example, PricewaterhouseCoopers has developed the "K factor", a model that calculates the amount of knowledge entering and leaving the organisation. Due diligence teams will probably gain a degree of access to these types of knowledge audits, especially when such resources may significantly affect a business's purchase price.

Managerial capability

This constitutes both the intellectual and emotional capital of a business. The courtship process should help reveal the calibre of a firm's senior managers and confirm whether they have the energy and vision to drive the new business after the merger. Their skills and style can also be tested by sharing some of the results of the due diligence process, although this needs to be handled diplomatically and constructively. The reaction of managers can give useful insights into how they might behave when they belong to a bigger organisation, for example:

- Management style: is their style autocratic or participative?
- Openness versus defensiveness: do they attempt to explain away issues or ambiguities or push them under the carpet, or are they willing to discuss and explore the issues?
- Ability to see the big picture: are they parochial in their thinking and stuck in a small-business mentality, or can they view their business in a wider, perhaps international, context?
- Willingness to change: do they appear open to change, for example, acknowledging that something could be done better or differently, or perhaps done away with altogether? Do there appear to be many "sacred cows" indicated by comments such as "we have always done that", or "we couldn't possible change that"?
- Change-management skills: have they gone through rapid change themselves? Have they been involved in any significant change process, such as other M&As, delayering exercises, corporate turnarounds or helping create a joint venture or spin-off? Have they worked in different corporate environments and learnt to adapt their management style?

The more dependent on its human capital a firm is, the more important it is to extend the due diligence analysis to the second tier of management, to functional specialists and to people with under-exploited skills. When Lincoln Life Insurance acquired Cigna's individual life insurance and annuity business in 1997, the merger team placed a high priority on the retention of valued employees. Mike Walter, then chief integration officer, explains:

> At our initial meeting with Cigna ... here in Philadelphia, we went through the organisational chart line by line and said: "Who are the key players we need to ensure that we keep?"

Jon Boscia, Lincoln Life Insurance's CEO, declares:

> Getting the key employee list is extraordinarily important because in the business we are in, the value of the business is in the people. You can pay a lot of money and still go down the tubes if you don't get the people you need. It's very hard to figure out who the key people are when you are doing a carve-out rather than buying a whole company. You just don't know who is who, and they might not be on the organisational charts, as many of the key people are in shared service organisations outside the dedicated unit. So you really have to dig in.[6]

Cultural audits

Probably the greatest aid to understanding the nature and value of corporate personality has been the development of cultural audits. However, most of these audits simply examine the company's predominant values, beliefs and behaviours to help predict the degree of compatibility between the prospective partners. It is rare for an audit to explore culture as an integral aspect of a company's worth and as a source of competitive advantage that must be protected and harnessed during a merger or acquisition.

Management writers and consultants Charles Hampden-Turner and Fons Trompenaars are among those trying to get managers to view their companies differently. Their starting point is the belief that "a company is a living system, with its own sense of direction and integrity". They believe that this uniqueness is all too often destroyed during an M&A and that "in most cases, the company ... actually loses value within days or weeks of being acquired".

This loss of value is mainly the result of a misunderstanding or mis-management of the very quality that helped make a business successful in the first place (see "Perils of acquisition" below). The two consultants recommend that companies should adopt a "strategy of acclimatisation" by taking a "policy of minimalism ... at any rate until you have studied and learned how and why your acquisition became successful enough to attract you".[7]

Mr Hampden-Turner and Mr Trompenaars work with the acquired company's management team to produce a "narrative history" of the company. Through discussions, they identify the various crises that have helped shape the business and conduct in-depth interviews to discover:

> ... what visions and aspirations those running the company entertain. Since the acquirer brings new capital, those visions are sometimes ambitious and exciting. We then study how the acquired company's reporting systems can, with the fewest possible changes, be adapted to the information the parent wants to achieve.

The parent should only take control, if this is appropriate, once it has "internalised" the other partner's way of working.

Perils of acquisition

Charles Hampden-Turner and Fons Trompenaars argue that the "living system" of an acquired company soon begins to "wilt" if the acquirer is too heavy-handed and anxious to take control as soon as possible. Ideally, both partners should aim to "ride high" by reconciling their skills and learning from each other. Instead, the following scenarios occur.

- **A bear hug.** "The life is squeezed out" of an acquired company when its bigger parent imposes its bureaucracy upon it. Founders may leave, but even when they stay "the zest has likely gone out of their activities". The acquired company may believe that the new procedures are inappropriate and that its new parent does not understand it.
- **Preserved life stock.** The acquired company relinquishes its independence but receives little in return. It is "corralled and segregated" by its new owner. Especially vulnerable "is the creativity of smaller companies", which can no longer retain their ability to remain "close to their customers, fleet of foot, fast

to respond ... Huge energies are absorbed by the incorporation, or by trying to resist its worst effects".

◪ **Runaway company.** The parent company tries to take control of an acquisition that is "more dynamic, smarter and closer to the leading edge than its parent". The acquisition, often a highly specialised niche player (they give the example of Barclays Bank's acquisition of BZW, an investment bank) proves "unruly and impetuous". The parent company expends much energy and time into trying to control its acquisition.

A small number of management consultancies are currently developing cultural due diligence that attempts to expose the linkages between corporate culture and competitive advantage. Perhaps the most comprehensive is a cultural audit based on 12 dimensions developed by Watson Wyatt.

1 **Strategic direction**, including:
   ◪ the company's "primary value propositions";
   ◪ the main drivers behind its strategy;
   ◪ the way these are expressed to customers and employees through its mission, vision and values.

2 **Key measures and definitions of success**, including:
   ◪ how key performance measurements are expressed, defined and communicated;
   ◪ the importance of customer requirements;
   ◪ which part of the business is responsible for managing and measuring performance;
   ◪ how these metrics are linked to rewards and incentives.

3 **Structure and protocols**, including:
   ◪ organisational basis, such as functional, geographical, matrix or business units;
   ◪ how staff and line units interact with each other and exchange communication, services and resources.

4 **Planning and control**, including:
   ◪ nature and importance of formal and informal processes;
   ◪ how staff are involved in strategic planning and budgeting;

- how decisions are made and the degree of consensus or autonomy expected;
- nature and limits of managerial authority.

5 **Employee engagement**, including:
- extent of employee involvement in special committees, task-forces and social events;
- use and extent of team working;
- balance between individual autonomy and group responsibility;
- linkages between individual performance and the business plan.

6 **Use and philosophy of information technology,** including:
- nature of technology platforms and architecture;
- how technology is used to leverage staff expertise and increase productivity;
- nature and level of IT skills.

7 **Physical environment**, including:
- the "look and feel" of offices;
- dress code;
- open-plan or private offices;
- impact of the environment on how work is done.

8 **Historical issues and expectations**, including:
- the best and worst events that helped shape the organisation;
- perceptions and obstacles that staff and managers will carry over to the new organisation;
- icons, images, incentives, opportunities and norms that staff will have a stake in preserving.

9 **Organisation-wide information transfer**, including:
- how different types of information are disseminated throughout the organisation;
- internal communication channels, programmes and media;
- what information is usually communicated or held back;
- employee cynicism or trust in internal communication.

10 **Information transfer between and among individuals**, including:
- formal or informal communications between and among staff and departments;

- face-to-face or written communication, feedback and instructions;
- direct or indirect access to bosses.

11 **Behaviour of leaders and managers**, including:
- typical boss/subordinate relationship;
- managerial style – coaching (providing informal help with professional development to individuals and teams) and facilitating, or traditional command and control;
- how leadership skills are identified, communicated and developed.

12 **Human capital**, including:
- the position and standing of human resources – strategic partner or administrative unit;
- HR's ability to affect organisational change;
- organisation's relationship with employees, including reward and benefits.

Cross-cultural audits

In cross-border M&As, cultural analysis is difficult and cross-cultural experts should be brought in to help. An interesting approach has been developed by the UK's Henley Management College, which attempts to build cultural profiles based on corporate culture, national culture and business culture (see below).

Intercultural analysis in M&As

Henley Management College uses a simple methodology with companies considering cross-border M&As and joint ventures. Executives can fill in a questionnaire that helps analyse the culture of their company and the business culture of their country. For example, participants are asked whether their country appears to give greater emphasis to social benefits or to capitalist values. Is their company "long sighted" or a "prisoner of the past"? Companies use these results to explore cross-cultural compatibility with potential foreign partners.

Terry Garrison, who developed the tool, explains:

> It identifies how people, money and time are managed in a company, the business customs of a country and how its politics, economics, religion and history impact on the way business is done".[8]

Mr Garrison believes that "intercultural analysis" should be a strategic factor in M&AS and JVs, and that it would have helped DaimlerChrysler anticipate the huge differences in the way the two companies negotiated with their workforces and the wider economic differences in how American and German banks support cross-border mergers.

Human-resources due diligence

Many managers understandably believe that human capital is covered by a human-resources due diligence, but this is often not the case, as Jerry Paten, a consultant, points out (see "M&A insights" below). HR due diligence is often conducted by lawyers and financial specialists who primarily focus on the contractual obligations and financial costs and implications of HR, including:

- employment terms and conditions;
- pension-scheme arrangements;
- reward systems and performance management;
- demographic information about staff, such as gender, age profile, tenure, location, turnover.

This information, essential as it is, is likely to yield little insight into how much the business's human capital (as opposed to human resources) supports the business and is itself a source of added value. A growing number of companies are giving responsibility for issues concerning human capital to knowledge directors, even though they arguably belong to strategic human-resources management and/or organisational development (for an example, see Paul Greenwood's description of knowledge management in "M&A insights" on the next page).

M&A INSIGHTS

Jerry Paton, a consultant at Penna, who has experiences of mergers from working as a human-resources manager at Nationwide Building Society and then as human-resources director at Occles

"I have found that due diligence is very finance driven, although there is now a greater understanding and awareness that what looks good on paper in terms of historic financial figures will not necessarily translate into future success because the companies may not work together successfully. Success is more than a shallow degree of collaboration between two companies. It hinges upon people working together and blending their cultures and behaviours.

"My early experiences were that HR was given the due diligence data just to ensure that we got everyone on the payroll. Typically, one would read various paragraphs saying there seems to be a good fit between the two companies. However, there would be little evidence of anyone systematically analysing the nature of this fit. Even today, few due diligence teams consider the embedded values and cultures of the organisations or ask what the issues are. They rarely try to assess whether successful integration will depend on a significant investment in organisation development. In all my years of working in HR, I don't recall ever seeing that type of approach.

"In reality, HR ends up doing cultural audits after the deal goes through. You can then face a lot of problems. For example, many of the people we acquired at Occles were academically brilliant, but the business needed them to adopt a different set of behaviours. We needed more commercial awareness throughout the organisation – these people just didn't have these qualities and they had no intention of changing.

"I think due diligence must address cultures and values in a more systematic and analytical way. However, if you are doing things behind closed doors, it is more difficult to do a cultural audit. But this is a real test for the top team – they should know what the embedded cultural values are; they should know what the people issues are. In reality, many senior managers find it easier to talk about the finances and the IT systems etc. Yet it is now recognised that organisational success does not depend on having the best structures or processes or people; it is how these single elements combine that really counts. Due diligence often pays lip service to these issues yet they are not fully analysed or understood. It is also rare to find an HR professional on the due diligence team who has the power and clout to say 'I have real reservations about this deal because of a specific people issue'."

M&A INSIGHTS

Paul Greenwood, director of knowledge, Clifford Chance, describes how knowledge management can help harness the skills of the merged firm's 7,000 lawyers and support staff around the world

"The value placed on a company is now much more related to its intangible assets – its knowledge, skills, brands and customer relationships. Our goal is to ensure that every client feels it has the amassed knowledge of an international integrated law firm working on its problem, not just the particular lawyer it is working with. Knowledge management makes the difference.

"I see knowledge management as a four-stage process: first, making facts and data widely available; second, ensuring key lessons are learnt – for example, through systematically reviewing a transaction to see what lesson can be learnt; third, making best practice available to everyone with the best thinking and processes; and, finally, the big prize, where a firm is routinely creating leading-edge thinking.

"But knowledge management goes further. For us, it is about redefining the role of the lawyer and what the lawyer does for the client and about rethinking the whole way we do business. Online advisory services knowledge will free lawyers to do more interesting work. New career paths should open for our support staff. We are already seeing a 'middle office' develop through the emergence of interdisciplinary specialist and hybrid roles, for example in information technology, which is breaking down traditional barriers between lawyers and support staff."

The emotional capital of brands

Companies started putting a value on brands in their balance sheets some 20 years ago. But the art of attributing an accurate value to a brand is a fine one. The due diligence process can help uncover customer perceptions about a company's brands and their underlying strengths, yet it explores less frequently the attitude and degree of loyalty of employees to the branded goods they make and sell. Brand loyalty can become a major issue after a merger, especially if the incoming new management team is insensitive to employees' feelings.

This was an issue recognised with hindsight when Glaxo acquired Wellcome. Although the name of the company became Glaxo Wellcome, many Wellcome people felt that the identity of Wellcome had been given short shrift. Elaine Davis, director of human-resources services at Glaxo Wellcome Inc, an American subsidiary of Glaxo Wellcome, comments:

> From my perspective as a Glaxo person (the merger) was inspiring; it was exciting to think that we would be building a company like no other in the industry. So it was hard for me to understand sometimes why my Wellcome counterparts were so unhappy ... many of them have been employed far longer than Glaxo people, and there's a significant amount of name identification, brand identification with their company. And the loss of that, I think, was just very painful for them.[9]

Competition complications

Running alongside due diligence is the process of receiving regulatory approval in link-ups that result in a "concentration" of competition in a specific business sector, where a merged business is perceived to be so dominant within its market that it hurts competition.

Notification of a merger or acquisition must be given to trade regulatory bodies. In the UK, this is the Office of Fair Trading, which, if it is concerned about the deal, refers it to the Competition Commission (formerly the Mergers and Monopolies Commission), which then investigates the deal for a period of three to six months. In the EU, the European Commission has a Merger Task Force to oversee M&AS. In America, the Securities and Exchange Commission (SEC) is the body that decides on antitrust matters. The legal complexities of this process are outside the remit of this book, but below is a rundown of what is involved in M&AS referred to the EU authorities.

Procedure for M&As in the EU

- A company submits its proposal in the shape of Form CO, a lengthy document that requires companies to supply extensive and detailed information about their mode of operation, the structure of their current markets and potentially "affected markets".
- The European Commission considers these proposals and decides whether to launch a formal investigation. In all cases that do not involve "serious doubt", a clearance decision is taken within one month from notification.
- The Commission begins an in-depth investigation, lasting four months. Companies have until 90 days after the Commission launches its probe to offer solutions to potential competition problems.
- The Commission puts in writing its assessment of a merger and its recommendations.
- This report is forwarded to members of the EU's merger advisory committee. This also consults experts from all 15 EU states before taking a final decision.

AstraZeneca's Ms May speaks of dealing with the EU's Merger Task Force:

The Task Force was concerned about the sale and decided to launch a full-scale investigation. It requires a phenomenal amount of effort from people to gather the data required by the Task Force. The relevant data existed within Zeneca, but not necessarily in the right form. I had to mobilise many different people within the agrochemicals division to help assemble the numbers. The Task Force tends to respond very quickly with a host of detailed supplementary questions that we were required to answer within tight timescales. We also had to attend a number of meetings in Brussels. The Merger Task Force people were very cordial but very assertive and demanding.

Even when the investigation proceeds smoothly, managers still need to be on hand to provide guidance to the team that is liaising directly with antitrust officials. Ms May says:

It makes a tremendous difference to have easy access to senior managers. There are times when you need their input very quickly, and we certainly received a lot of support from key Zeneca managers during the whole process of selling the agrochemical division.

If the authorities respond unfavourably to a proposed merger, the managers involved are likely find themselves on a plane to Brussels. For example, when GE proposed a $43 billion merger with its rival Honeywell, the former's CEO, Jack Welch, had to attend a number of lengthy meetings with Mario Monti, the EU antitrust chief, and his team of lawyers and advisers. Mr Welch first tried to head off a formal investigation by personally pleading the merits of the link-up. His attempt failed, leading to a series of tense meetings where the Commission argued that the combination of GE's power in the market for aircraft jet engines and Honeywell's strengths in avionics would give it a near-monopoly in the market for jet engines for large commercial and regional aircraft. Despite all these efforts and significant managerial attention, the deal was finally rejected.

Mr Monti said the divergent ruling was partly caused by GE notifying the Commission much later than the American antitrust authorities. The deal was vetoed on the grounds that it would damage competition in the European aerospace sector. Mr Monti criticised the two companies for being unwilling to make what he considered as "modest remedies". The

Merger Task Force wanted GE to partially float GE Capital Aviation Services and Honeywell to sell some of its avionics business, but the two companies refused, arguing that these divestments would negate the reason for the merger. In September 2001, GE and Honeywell separately launched appeals against the decision.

Because of the increase in the number of incomplete or incorrect merger notifications (through completing a Form CO), the EU has developed the following best-practice guidelines in consultation with the Merger Task Force.

- It is always appropriate even in straightforward cases to have pre-notification contacts with the Merger Task Force case team. Notifying parties should submit a briefing memorandum at least three working days before a first meeting. This first meeting should take place preferably at least one to two weeks before the expected date of notification. In more difficult cases, a more protracted pre-notification period may well be appropriate.

- Following this first meeting, the parties should provide before notification the Merger Task Force with a substantially complete draft Form CO. The Merger Task Force should be given in general one week to review the draft before a further meeting or being asked to comment on the phone on the adequacy of the draft.

- At pre-notification meetings, a discussion should take place on what should and should not be included in the notification. Indeed, it may not be necessary to provide all information specified in Form CO. However, all requests to omit any part of the information specified should be discussed in detail and agreed with the Merger Task Force.

- Potentially affected markets should be openly discussed with the case team in good faith, even if the notifying parties take a different view on market definition. Furthermore, wherever there may be uncertainty or differences of view over market definitions, it will be more prudent to produce market shares on one or more alternative bases – eg, by national markets as well as by an EU-wide one.

- Notifying parties and their advisers should take care to ensure that the information contained in Form CO has been carefully prepared and verified. Contact details for customers and competitors should be carefully checked to ensure that the Merger Task Forces' investigations are not delayed.

◪ At meetings in general (both at the pre-notification stage and during notification), it is preferable that cases are discussed with both legal advisers and business representatives who have a good understanding of the relevant markets.

Provided these guidelines are complied with, the Merger Task Force case team will in principle be prepared to confirm informally the adequacy of a draft notification at the pre-notification stage or, if appropriate, to identify in what specific respects it is incomplete.

Negotiating the deal
The results of due diligence have an important impact on negotiations as these will have a direct bearing on the price, terms and deal structure of the M&A, which will hinge on:

◪ price;
◪ acquired assets and business units;
◪ assumption of debt;
◪ employee liabilities;
◪ tax arrangements and indemnities;
◪ the performance of the new business;
◪ the arrangement for the transfer of shares;
◪ the bridging arrangements for a variety of staff or functions, such as continuing to supply IT support for a specific period of time until a shared systems interface is implemented.

In almost any deal, financial and legal advisers will play a big role in negotiating (in practice agreeing) the basic details, but no firm should delegate the job of formulating the final negotiating strategy or the job of ensuring that the agreements are in keeping with the original vision and objectives of the M&A.

The actions and behaviours that are most likely to kill a deal are:

◪ failing to continue to communicate with the potential partner throughout detailed negotiations;
◪ failing to follow up speedily on promises;
◪ answering questions too slowly;
◪ constantly introducing new elements in the contract;
◪ coming in with an inadequate offer;
◪ promising cash and later offering a cash/share deal;

- being too keen or sending the wrong signals and so generating unreasonable expectations about the deal offer;
- assuming the deal is done when a verbal agreement is made – senior managers should remain involved to the point when the agreement is signed.

Maintaining momentum is often cited as the most critical factor in reaching the altar. Laurence Mellman, WPP's director of special projects, says:

> Delay kills, especially when it is due to bureaucracy. It is bound to dilute some of the joy for the owner/manager if, after committing to the deal, the whole thing goes through a committee stage for the next six months. It works well if the principals can agree on the broad brush strokes and have people underneath to work out the detail.

Mike Walsh, Ogilvy & Mather's CEO (Europe, Middle East and Africa), also emphasises the need for speed:

> If the target company is good, it will inevitably be in competition with someone else. Moreover, if the deal is done quickly, it makes a positive statement about the larger group they are joining and its eagerness to have them.

The manager of a media relations business supplies the following advice:

> Negotiations can be confrontational at times. My role is to act as an intermediary when discussions come to a stop because of "insurmountable" issues. If you are directly involved in negotiations, the selling party has nowhere else to appeal. You must stay out of it, or you will have a post-acquisition job to do.

Bill Womack, CEO of Landmark, a business broker based in America, specialises in negotiating sales of owner/managed businesses. He strongly believes that owners should not sit in during negotiations to sell their business because of their emotional links to the business and the unrealistic value they often put on it. He advocates personality profile testing.

*It is very helpful if they understand their personality type and
how that affects their behaviour and how they respond to the
buyer's negotiating team. They need to understand their
preferences; for example, are they "analyticals" who need to
understand all the figures or they "drivers", people who want
to get things done, who see the big picture and don't bother
with details.*

If owner/managers can do this, "they can then begin to understand
what they need to do to meet the buyer's expectations and to avoid misunderstandings and conflict", he says.

Following successful negotiations, companies can announce the
banns in a formal "letter of intent", a non-binding understanding. This
typically contains:

- the reason for the M&A and predicted business benefits;
- proposed financial terms;
- terms and conditions;
- organisational and operational overview.

Managerial challenges during evaluation

This chapter has explored different ways of evaluating a merger or
acquisition. The attributes needed by managers to oversee that work
successfully are as follows.

- Competence in handling both "hard" quantitative data and "soft"
  qualitative information. Due diligence has traditionally
  concentrated on the elements of a business that can be measured
  and verified. This, together with the fact that specialists such as
  lawyers and investment bankers conduct the investigation,
  means there is often an unconscious concentration on codified
  information (that can be defended in court). Managers who focus
  on this type of information risk ignoring or overlooking richer
  and more qualitative information or insights. Competence in
  dealing with hard and soft information also requires the ability to
  be able to make decisions based on objective analysis and
  intuition.
- The ability to absorb the details while keeping a firm eye on the
  bigger picture. M&A evaluation will produce volumes, even
  roomfuls, of information. Managers must make the right

judgment about the depth of information needed for different aspects of due diligence. This is often hard and can become a major worry – especially when managers are operating to a tight deadline.

- The ability to judge when to accept uncertainty or ambiguity. Realistically, not every facet of a merger can be hammered out on paper. Managers must be able to discern which issues need to be tied up before the deal and which can be left to be clarified later.
- The ability to ascribe appropriate values to intangible as well as tangible assets.
- To be supportive and collaborative, even when due diligence uncovers weaknesses in the M&A partner. They must persuade their prospective partner to co-operate with due diligence – although some findings may need to be kept confidential, they should be open about the results of the investigation. Skilful "wooers" conduct these talks in a constructive manner that emphasises mutual learning and co-operation.

5 Creating a new nucleus: the integration process

A S THE LAWYERS and investment bankers pack their briefcases and leave, the managers who have been involved in the merger process may be forgiven for experiencing a sudden sense of panic. The heady euphoria generated by the ups and downs of making a deal often dissipates in the cold light of day when managers realise that they have now to decide how to handle the integration process. Most critical of all is the question of how they will live up to all the ambitious talk of growth and merger synergies. Much of M&A strategy following the announcement of a deal is emergent and on a "need to do" basis. The rigours of courting a partner, of being duly diligent and of closing the deal leaves little time for constructing a detailed practical plan of how to combine the two businesses.

The experience of Phil Radcliffe, strategic change director of Diageo, a consumer goods company, reflects that of many faced with making an M&A work:

> The integration process between Guinness and GrandMet, the two businesses that were combining parts of their drinks business to create UDV [Diageo is the holding company] started with a blank piece of paper. All our thinking had concentrated on resourcing the top team and striking the right balance in key appointments between Guinness and GrandMet. Early in the planning period for the implementation of the merger we became embroiled in discussions with LVMH, which owned 14.2% of Guinness and disagreed with the merger strategy. Announcing the link-up to the City had been a rigorous and exhausting process. After the merger was announced senior management were keen to celebrate the news, but their immediate reaction was: "How are we going to do this? What does it mean for the business?" They wanted the detail, but no one had yet had the chance to think through properly how we were going to do it.

Integration planning is one of the most difficult tasks of a successful merger or acquisition. In a matter of weeks, merger teams must process the information from due diligence and develop an integration process that will help ensure that merger synergies are delivered to a tight timescale – or so the theory goes. Thus vague or generalised statements about complementary portfolios and capabilities must be translated into a set of specific priorities and actions, with detailed measurements and milestones.

The time delays between the announcement of and the completion of an M&A can be used for detailed integration planning – even though any delay in closure can cause serious problems. Because of wrangles with the antitrust authorities, the merger between AOL Time Warner took almost a year to go through, yet chairman Steve Case commented:

> In retrospect – even though we may have wished the merger process was a little more streamlined – we have been able to use the year constructively to think about how to operate this new company in a new way and to build alignment among the executives.

PricewaterhouseCoopers, the result of the merger between accountancy firms Price Waterhouse and Coopers & Lybrand in June 1998, used the nine months before it gained regulatory approval in America and the EU to design much of the structure of the new business and to select the top two management tiers of the merged partnership. Ed Smith, responsible for global learning and education, comments:

> It was unnerving waiting for clearance, especially because two other global consultancies announced their intention to merge and we were worried that this would spoil our pitch. However, our integration team refused to take the foot off the pedal and continued on the basis that we would complete the merger in June 1998 as expected.

(For an overview of PricewaterhouseCoopers's merger and integration approach see "Speed counts" on page 127.)

Integration planning: a critical success factor

M&A studies reveal that merger success is closely linked with effective integration planning before the deal is completed, as the following examples show.

◧ Mercer Management Consulting, *Making mergers work for*

profitable growth: the importance of pre-deal planning about post-deal management, 1997:

> The improved performance of the deals of the 1990s are not explained by price ... The data show no direct correlation [between] better strategy and better returns ... Success over the long haul results from having a comprehensive post-merger management programme that develops and broadcasts a vision for the new company, creates a new organisation by aligning the components with the vision, and promotes a speedy integration based on vision and alignment. The earlier and more thoroughly that programme is mapped, the greater the odds of ultimate success.

◪ University of Edinburgh Management School and PA Consulting Group, *Creating shareholder value from acquisition integration,* 2000:

> One of the survey's less surprising results was that planning and programme management are vital to a successful integration. PA's findings clearly indicate that early implementation planning is worth the effort, even if the information available prior to completion is difficult to obtain. Improved returns were found for companies that established an integration plan and an integration team before completion.

◪ Watson Wyatt, *Assessing and Managing Human Capital,* 1999:

> The key to successful integration is a systematic, thorough and expedient process.

Integration planning is piecemeal planning

However, these surveys reveal that integration planning is often poor. In some instances, managers are unprepared for many of the problems and issues they have to confront after the merger announcement (see Chapter 6). Another reason appears to be that companies are simply poor at change management and project management, two skills at the heart of effective integration planning. For example, the University of Edinburgh Management School/PA Consulting survey revealed that companies placed much higher priority on budgeting and cost control during their integration efforts than they did on change and risk management. In a follow-up survey in 2001, PA found that despite the acknowledged importance of integration planning and management, only 14% of North European (French, Benelux, German and Scandinavian) respondents established a "programme office" specifically to manage their M&A integration. In certain aspects of integration planning, such as risk management and change management, they showed "a greater reliance on a more informal approach".

A survey of the technology, media and communications sector by Andersen, an international accounting and consulting firm, reveals a piecemeal and inconsistent approach to merger planning and integration. A staggering 75% of managers from 31 of the largest companies in the sector involved in M&As admitted they did not follow "a clear, consistent process for the integration phase of transactions". They highlighted the following problems, most of which were people-based:

- inertia;
- lack of solidarity;
- poor identification of issues;
- bad communication;
- lack of clarity.

John Ormerod, managing partner of Andersen UK, explains:

> [The piecemeal approach to M&As] stems from a belief among executives that "every deal is different" and that the development of a clear policy, therefore, is either impossible or inadvisable. For me personally, the most surprising thing was the lack of surprise among the executives. It seems extraordinary that while the average company has plenty of procedures for buying stationery or for travel etc, few have organised and formal processes for managing their M&A activity.

(For a notable exception, see the example of GE Capital, GE's financial services business, below.)

GE Capital finds the path to integration enlightenment

In a seminal paper on M&A integration,[1] GE Capital explained how its acquisition of Gelco during the mid-1980s became a "watershed", as the company embraced "a new way of thinking about acquisitions – a recognition that there were predictable issues that could be anticipated long before the deal actually closes".

Almost by accident, GE Capital realised that the integration framework that it had developed for the Gelco acquisition could be applied equally well to its other acquisitions. Many of these deals came in "different shapes and sizes", such as:

◪ "portfolio or asset purchases", that add volume to a business without adding people;

◪ "consolidating acquisitions", where an acquired business is added into an existing GE Capital business;

◪ "platform" or strategic acquisitions, where the acquisition operates in a sector that is new to GE Capital;

◪ "hybrid" purchases, where parts of the acquisition are slotted into one or several GE Capital businesses while other parts become joint ventures or remain stand-alone operations.

GE Capital calls its framework the "Pathfinder model", whereby the M&A process is divided into four distinct "action stages", each of which is subdivided into specific subprocesses and then illustrated with examples of best practices that integration managers can consider using. The company continues to work on the framework through periodic internal conferences and forums where different teams discuss their M&A experience, refine best practices and share effective tools and processes. GE Capital stresses that M&A "competence is something never fully attained, that it is only the jumping-off point for an ever higher standard".

In a sense, the framework is both holistic and situational. Merger teams have an overall framework for developing an integration plan yet retain the freedom to choose the practices that are best suited to helping them fulfil the strategic goals of the M&A and its degree of operational linkage with GE Capital. In holistic terms, Pathfinder advocates a number of guiding principles, including the following.

◪ In the pre-acquisition phase, as much attention is placed on cultural issues as on the business case. Cultural assessment and issues of cultural compatibility receive high priority. Integration planning starts as soon as possible.

◪ In the "foundation building" phase, the emphasis is on the importance of managers of both GE Capital and the firm that has been acquired working jointly on an integration plan.

◪ The implementation phase should be rapid and involve continual assessment of progress and adjustment of the integration plan.

◪ Post-implementation, viewed as the "assimilation" phase where the integration effort is assessed, the long-term business plan is further refined and evaluated.

Mr Ormerod talks of a widespread failure to engage employees during the integration process:

> *Such poor integration planning is even more surprising when you think that when you do an acquisition, you are selling yourself as well as buying another company. Success comes from making the whole worth more than the sum of its parts, so you are trying to engage the other people in various forms of added value activity, so it is something you are doing with them, not doing to them. So the challenge is to create an integration approach that is not adversarial but something that engages people. I don't believe that today's companies are locked in the adversarial model, I just think they have not thought through how to engage their people in value-adding activities and then developed this into a process for* M&AS.

A survey of 53 companies by The Conference Board, a global business network and research organisation, revealed similar findings, prompting the author, Stephen Gates, to comment:

> *Since integrating an acquisition or merger can provoke major change and result in downsizing, many companies prefer to consider the process a one-time ordeal.*[2]

Some 55% of respondents said their company had not been able to transform their M&A experiences into a core competency, enabling them to think about merger integration as a planned process.

This piecemeal approach to M&A integration is reflected in the wide variety of integration processes used by companies around the world. The 2001 PA Consulting study supplies a useful overview of integration approaches. For instance:

- 53% of respondents say they have a integration plan prior to completion.
- 37% of respondents develop their plan post-completion.
- 45% form an integration team before completion.
- 40% form a team after completion.
- Planning horizons for integration vary widely. There is no evidence to suggest that one particular integration timescale (for example, the concept of the "100 day" plan that has been

promoted by merger specialists in recent years) is judged as optimal.

◪ There is a spectrum of integration management structures, with no clear evidence indicating that one structure is more successful than another.

The spectrum of integration management structures identified by PA ranges from a "single accountability model" to a "line accountability model", with a number of "hybrids and variants" in between. The single accountability model is where a single director is appointed to champion the integration process and drive the agreed plan from a central point of contact. The line accountability model is where integration is pushed down the line. Business divisions and subsidiaries are responsible for integration, so this process is part of a line manager's job and is not conducted by a dedicated team.

The PA study emphasises that both models appear equally effective and are used to handling differing degrees of integration. The companies studied for this book have adopted a range of integration approaches, and this chapter contains illustrations of both centralised and decentralised approaches.

Successful integration: more than project management

Both the PA study and The Conference Board report suggest that successful integration depends on the ability of business leaders to develop core competencies in this area so that they can formulate a coherent approach to integration. But as James Crowley, head of the UK strategy and business architecture division at Accenture, a management and technology services organisation, comments:

> *Many managers have experienced only one or two mergers.*
> *They often go into crisis mode when they begin to plan how to*
> *integrate their businesses. More experienced companies tend to*
> *have developed a carefully worked machine that enables a*
> *small number of people to proceed smoothly with the task of*
> *integration.*

A "crisis" mentality stems from the assumption that the merger being undertaken is an isolated event and idiosyncratic in nature. This encourages managers to assume that they simply have to survive the short-term disruption of bolting the combination together, after which it is just a matter of sorting out "soft" issues after integration when the merged company settles into a state of "business as usual". M&As are, therefore, almost always viewed as disruptive and painful events, rather like taking a nasty dose of medicine in order to return to good health.

This mindset is seen in the perspective of Bill Swanson, CEO of Raytheon Systems, who told the PA researchers:

> The real key is you do your planning, you make your hard
> decisions and you do them all at once. It's like the old thing
> with the band-aid, you can pull it off slowly, or you can pull it
> off quick. It is better to do it quick.

Many companies, especially American ones, follow this approach and design an integration process that aims to create operational linkages, such as new accounting processes, an integrated management structure, shared IT platform and so on, all within a military-style campaign of operation – often within "100 days". Lucent Technologies, a telecommunications and computing company, for instance, has designed an integration programme that aims for completion 100 days after the M&A announcement. Every integration activity is assigned a stretching "speed goal". For example, the following should all be completed by or at the closure of the deal:

- channel strategy and account planning;
- logo and sign changes;
- month-end accounting procedures.

Typically, companies then roll out a series of workshops and training events that may examine cultural issues or discuss a new set of values and behaviours with the aim of unifying the new company. The human-resources director of an international retailing business that took such an approach comments:

> Our executive board took a serious approach to cultural
> integration and developed a new set of values and operating
> principles. But that was driven as an intellectual staff exercise
> and, with hindsight, we realised that "launching" a set of values
> did not achieve much. We needed to find ways to energise the
> employees of both organisations to get into the whole culture

issue as it connected with them and their experiences and their
new relationships during the integration process.

Within this paradigm, M&A integration is essentially the same as managing a large, complex project. The managerial challenge is to break down the integration into a series of tasks, each with their own set of accountabilities, milestones and critical success factors. Integration is fundamentally an operational matter, and success is defined by whether and when the project teams attain their objectives. When they do, the integration office is closed and the management formally announces that the two organisations have been successfully integrated.

The DaimlerChrysler merger that took place in 1998 is a salutary example of the shortcomings of this approach. By any yardstick, the merger has proved disastrous, with operating losses estimated at more than $2 billion in 2001, a year the company announced cuts of more than 19,000 jobs. Yet DaimlerChrysler's integration process appeared masterly in its execution. Following a meeting lasting only 17 minutes where the two CEOs agreed a merger and a rapid negotiating period of four months, the combining automobile businesses maintained the pace by finishing their integration programme in a mere 12 months, a year ahead of schedule.

In terms of skilful project management, the DaimlerChrysler merger cannot be faulted. A core of 12 "issue resolution teams" (IRTs) co-ordinated 98 main projects, which spawned a further 1,200 specific projects. The IRTs monitored progress through a newly created post-merger integration Infobase. This comprised 100 databases containing information about individual projects and tracked their progress against financial and non-financial performance targets using a "traffic-light" system of green, yellow and red. Any integration-team leader whose project entered the red zone faced the prospect of having to account in person to the board.

In the event, the integration projects reached their targets, but the end product was patently not an integrated global business. As *The Economist* reported on November 25th 2000:

Cumbrous working parties toiled away melding Teutonic with
American methods of running meetings and reaching
decisions. There was much talk of "one company, two head
offices" – all of it nonsense. In the end, both parties agreed to
live and let live. But they should have been trying to yoke

*together their engineering and product-development work
rather than running Chrysler as a separate division. In the
event, DaimlerChrysler got the worst of both worlds. There
was no synergy between the two arms, and Chrysler's
management problem grew unheeded. Carping criticism from
head-office in Stuttgart persuaded fed-up Chrysler executives
to leave for new jobs, further weakening the company.*

Another serious drawback of viewing M&As as painful, private and one-off events is that organisational and personal learning can be stopped in their tracks. In interviews, managers of successful M&As frequently described experiences that had given them valuable insights about personal and organisational change and transformation. These experiences included M&As that were quite unlike others they had been involved in, such as business restructurings, or the creation of a strategic alliance or a joint venture.

Daigeo's Mr Radcliffe speaks of his experience of the merger between United Distillers and GrandMet's International Distillers Vintners. He comments:

*When we first met with managers from GrandMet, we
assumed that they had much more expertise in handling a
merger than we did. But as we began the process of integrating
the two businesses, we began to realise that much of what we
had learnt about change was directly applicable to mergers.
My advice to managers thinking about a merger is not to
discount the skills and disciplines and learning about change
that already exists in their organisations. This was a powerful
insight for us to take into our more recent merger in 2000,
when we decided to merge UDV with Guinness Brewing and
then subsequently with Seagrams to create Diageo, a global
beverage alcohol business.*

The widespread tendency to think about M&A integrations as large, complex projects is a necessary but not sufficient approach. The great strength of project management is that it enables huge change projects to be packed into discrete activities and managed to a tight timescale – an essential prerequisite of any successful combination. But if the sole approach to integration is project-based, people are encouraged to believe that:

- integration is an end point;
- integration is measurable and quantifiable;
- definitions of success revolve around completing tasks and achieving tangible goals;
- operational and organisation issues must be more important than culture;
- integration is solutions oriented;
- differences between the merging businesses are problems (rather than opportunities for learning) that need to be resolved and eliminated.

Project-based integration rests on the assumption that the end point (however defined, however sensible) is all important, and that the pain and disruption along the way needs to be avoided, minimised, or anaesthetised through better project management and human-resource management. This may be overstating it, but the important point is that project-based integration carries a whole set of messages and values at an almost subliminal level.

These unconscious messages may prevent employees moving through the stages of co-operation, collaboration and commitment, which are the routes to a successful M&A. Anything that does not fit easily into a project-based approach gets overlooked or sidelined. How can you justify allocating time and resources to – or even raise – such issues, measured against the priorities of the integration timetable? Against this backdrop, the necessary processes of disclosure and debate, the essential components of engagement, are stillborn.

For example, when Lloyds TSB acquired Scottish Widows in 1999, it decided to adopt certain parts of Scottish Widows's IT systems. Following that decision, Lloyds TSB shifted much of its IT resource to Scotland. According to a systems developer, the bank effected a smooth transition in terms of processes and people, yet it paid little attention to how these changes were perceived by its own IT employees. He recalls:

> It felt like a reverse takeover to us. The worst aspect of
> adopting their software was that many of us felt marginalised.
> My greatest anxiety was that I would be de-skilled and end up
> in a "career stopping" position. My manager's only concern
> was for the team to deliver various project deliverables on
> schedule so that he could gain his promotion.

Managers often realise retrospectively that their integration processes were not geared up to dealing with important issues of how to work together. For example, Stephen Dando, who was management development director at Diageo (now human-resources director at the BBC), speaks of the tendency of many managers to minimise the spectre of cultural differences when they make an M&A announcement. He says:

> With hindsight, I would certainly have wanted George Bull [the GrandMet chairman] and Tony Greener [chairman of Guinness] to have had considerably more input from our people about the statements that were made about Grand Met and Guinness having similar cultures. Without meaning to, these assertions made it illegitimate for people to discuss and explore differences.
>
> A much healthier launch would have been to say, "the good news is that our cultures are different, but we believe profoundly that they are complementary". A great starting point would have been for us to say that we recognise that our cultures are actually quite distinctive and in many ways quite different. We share many things in common but there are lots of differences. We want to celebrate those differences. We want to explore and understand those differences. We can only do that if we legitimise that exploration, so we challenge our senior executives to spend the next six months in a very robust debate with each other talking about those differences and comparing and contrasting how they do things. From the insights that flow, we will create a new culture. We will not rush at it, but we will draw a line under it at some point.

Expertise in project management certainly reduces the risk of failure but, on its own, does not necessarily increase the likelihood of success. Project-management-based integration will certainly result in the swift creation of new or shared processes or perhaps a new organisational structure. But it will not necessarily ensure that employees pool their knowledge, expertise and energy. In mergers where long-term success is dependent on creative collaboration across functional and organisational boundaries, something more is needed.

An integrated approach to integration

An integration process has a powerful impact on the culture, climate and personality of the emerging business. The way integration teams work across the combining organisations will strongly influence employees' views about what life will be like in the new business. If there is a severe disjunction between management messages and the way the integration teams work, then the vision for the combination will be undermined, even discredited. If employees are told that their expertise counts, and that their views and ideas are a valuable resource, they will expect opportunities to help build the new business. If they see integration teams being arrogant, high-handed, politically motivated, secretive or uninterested in any views except their own and those of their senior managers, then they will withdraw their support or actively resist the changes. What are the chances of collaboration when integration teams are positioned as experts, telling people what to do? Is mutual learning likely to occur when integration is conducted like a military campaign and integration teams act like paratroopers securing their base?

The more dependent on people an M&A is for its success, the more it needs to involve a people-based integration approach. To win people's hearts and minds, there must be a direct link between the M&A vision, the integration process and the emerging new business. The challenge is to develop integration processes that encourage employees and other important stakeholders to buy into the new business and to help deliver the full range of desired synergies – from day one.

Integration should be viewed as a unique and powerful opportunity decisively to change the organisational climate, culture and working practices of the combining organisations as the combination occurs, and not as a post-integration effort.

The disruption and uncertainty created by a merger, if managed correctly, can provide a window of opportunity to meld intellectual assets into new, value-creating combinations. Whether implemented by a centralised team or devolved to the line, the integration process should be:

- built on the principle of employee engagement, helping to create and nurture an ever widening sense of ownership and commitment to the new combination;
- tightly linked to the strategic vision and objectives of the M&A, ensuring they help build a platform for the successful leveraging of the human capital within the combining organisations;
- designed in such a way as to encourage dialogue, upward feedback and the flow of knowledge, ideas and fresh insights around the organisation;

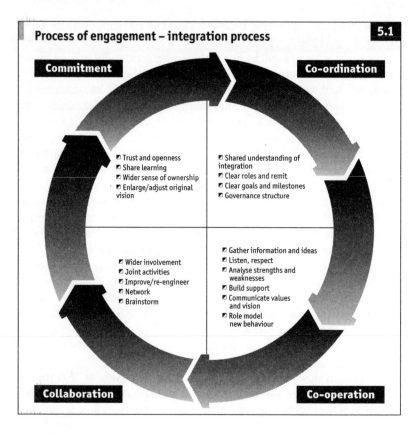

Process of engagement – integration process 5.1

Commitment
- Trust and openness
- Share learning
- Wider sense of ownership
- Enlarge/adjust original vision

Co-ordination
- Shared understanding of integration
- Clear roles and remit
- Clear goals and milestones
- Governance structure

Collaboration
- Wider involvement
- Joint activities
- Improve/re-engineer
- Network
- Brainstorm

Co-operation
- Gather information and ideas
- Listen, respect
- Analyse strengths and weaknesses
- Build support
- Communicate values and vision
- Role model new behaviour

- effective at feeding personal and collective learning into the continuing process of strategy formulation.

Chart 5.1 shows the link between employee engagement and the integration process.

The problem is that shared learning, commitment and vision are intangible and evolving, and they cannot be easily identified, analysed and measured through an integration process. Any integration effort that tries to help employees move through the stages of co-ordination, co-operation, collaboration and commitment must be able to have an impact on mindsets, values, perceptions and behaviours. This requires integration to be viewed as a psychological and cultural process as much as a series of tasks linking together various organisational resources. This view of integration does not invalidate a project-

Chart 5.2 **Approaches to integration**

Project-based integration	Engagement-based integration
Task oriented	Process oriented
Outputs/deliverables	Input
Operational/organisational focus	Cultural
Reach an end	Continuing, the journey itself is important
Stabilisation and closure	Creative destabilisation, evolving
Importance of expertise	Mindsets, behaviours, interpersonal skills
Solutions oriented	Two-way learning
Eliminate/resolve differences	Explore and exploit
Retrospective, post-event learning	Continuing learning and dissemination

management-based approach – it simply requires companies to balance formal disciplines with more process-oriented approaches throughout integration. In order to put both the "bones" of the new business in place, and to nurture the emerging "heart" and "brain" of its emotional and intellectual capital, as much attention needs to be given to what gets done as to how it gets done.

Chart 5.2 illustrates some of the shifts of emphasis that are required in order to use integration as a tool of engagement.

Build a shared understanding of what "integration" means

When the ultimate aim of a merger is to build a more collaboratively based business, it is logical that the integration process itself should be collaborative in its design and actively facilitate dialogue, mutual disclosure and mutual learning. However, in an M&A there is enormous pressure to be seen to be integrating operations and achieving "quick wins". There is therefore a powerful current towards focusing on tasks and tangible deliverables and away from seemingly less efficient approaches. If you want to build a new, collaborative business, you must swim against the current and ensure that integration activities are aligned with the type of business you are trying to build. The integration process itself becomes the foundation of the new business, helping to determine its shape, strength and durability.

The most important task for the leadership of any M&A is to build a shared vision of what it means to be integrated in a competitive context. Typically, M&A teams think of the end state of integration in the following terms.

- As a specific organisational model, for example, shifting from divisions based on geography to ones that concentrate on market sectors or product lines.
- When all overlapping or duplicating activities have been removed.
- When common controls, procedures and standards have been established.

But these definitions only touch upon the linkages an M&A may involve. Others might include the following.

- Operational: joint activities, for example, in areas such as procurement, manufacturing, production, sales and marketing, customer support, logistics.
- Financial: sharing financial assets to help spread risk and invest in further business development; installing financial measurements, taxation and accounting systems.
- Managerial: transferring managerial processes, disciplines and expertise between businesses or divisions; creating new managerial lines of accountability and responsibility; sharing human-resources management and training and development.
- Strategic: sharing competitive information, communicating strategy between business subsidiaries, jointly formulating strategy, or having input into the strategy and vision for the combined business.
- Knowledge: pooling expertise, experience and knowledge; coaching less capable divisions or subsidiaries; learning from subsidiaries operating in unfamiliar business sectors, geographical markets or emerging technologies; establishing common quality standards and procedures.

The logic and nature of these linkages should be driven by the synergies that the combination is aiming to achieve. However, integration extends beyond redesigned processes and structures. It also encapsulates a vision about the culture, climate, values and capabilities of the combined business – all the qualities that help ensure that people choose to engage with the combined business. This vision must be articulated at the earliest stage so that the integration team can ensure that the parameters and objectives of the various integration projects support this vision, rather than destroy it. Similarly, this vision can help guide the behaviour and attitudes of integration team members as they interact with different groups of employees throughout the business.

A document based on group-wide discussions among senior managers at advertising agency Ogilvy & Mather on what they have learnt about managing acquisitions asserts:

> *Acquisition integration is a process. It is a process by which an agency melds with another agency(ies) ... It is the creation of a new mindset". For Ogilvy & Mather, the essence of integration is about strengthening the group's innovative capability and its ability to deliver "360-degree" branding to customers.*

The document goes on to ask:

> *What is integration and what is it not? Integration is a catalyst of change ... It is not a set of established commonalities. Nor is it the institutionalisation of systems and procedures that obstruct the creative performance. Integration is not management control, but management support and coaching.*

Reaching a shared understanding of integration is particularly important in cross-border mergers. Before merging in January 2000, senior managers at law firms Clifford Chance, Pünder and Rogers & Wells worked to define integration in terms that were applicable to a variety of legal environments. Managers decided to focus on client relationships, as Michael Bray, the new firm's CEO, explains.

> *What is "integration" but getting people to work together to decide how best to deliver service to clients? The new firm's strategy is to deepen its relationships with major global clients and potential clients. The merger is an opportunity to make us do it and do it well, with decisions taken as close to the client as possible.*

UDV conducted a similar debate when it started looking at what it was trying to achieve through its integration programme. Senior managers discussed how the merger of Guinness's spirits division with the vodka and liqueurs business owned by GrandMet could lead to a genuine transformation of the business, not just in its organisational structure but also in its ability to pool market knowledge, create new products and develop new routes to markets. Mr Radcliffe explains:

We realised that what we wanted to achieve was not to integrate the two businesses, but to transform them completely. There was a great temptation internally to say "let's concentrate on integration for one and a half years or so and then in year three of the merger, let's aim for transformation".

However, our team of external consultants helped enormously by throwing down the challenge by suggesting that the merger wasn't about integration, it was about transformation. They discussed with us the strong likelihood that if we focused our efforts on integration only, there would be little energy left for transformation. We would be unable to mobilise the organisation for the next set of changes. We decided to "integrate with both eyes on transformation", which meant having transformation at the heart of our integration processes.

Diageo takes a decentralised approach to integration

The merger between the drinks businesses of GrandMet and Guinness was set in train when both companies decided that consolidation within the global spirits industry was inevitable and that a "first strike" merger would give them a substantial advantage over their competitors. The companies' CEOs had dinner together in April 1997 and quickly agreed to combine Guinness's drinks business, United Distillers (UD), with GrandMet's vodka and liqueurs business (owned by its subsidiary International Distillers and Vintners – IDV).

Shareholders of both companies gave their approval to the merger in November and American clearance was gained by December 1997. The merged group's holding company was named Diageo.

Diageo's new drinks business, UDV, started its life with two major advantages: a complementary set of branded spirits and a widely spread distribution network, with few overlaps. Guinness, for instance, had a strong presence in Asia and Latin America, as well as in its traditional markets (such as the UK and Ireland), and GrandMet's drinks business was strong in Europe (particularly Spain) and North America. Their branded spirits also created an enviable portfolio: GrandMet's well-known brands stretched from Smirnoff vodka to Bailey's liqueurs, and Guinness was strong in Scotch whisky (Johnnie Walker, Bell's, Classic Malts) and gins (Gordon's, Tanqueray).

As well as its physical assets – its distribution network and branded spirits – UDV perceived its intangible, intellectual assets to be the ability to create new drinks, and a close knowledge of local markets, especially in terms of consumer tastes and appropriate marketing approaches. The merged business was to harness these intellectual assets, as Phil Radcliffe, Diageo's director of strategic change, explains:

> Although GrandMet and Guinness had some marked differences in their cultures, both their strengths were in staying close to markets and making speedy decisions. In order to preserve these two things, we wanted to create a decentralised organisation, with significant autonomy going to the in-market national teams to deliver growth. We could have used a small central team to design a new organisational model and then replicated this across the 55 or so markets where we operated – just like cutting cookies. But we decided that we could not build a decentralised business using a centralised, integration effort.

Perhaps most importantly, asserts Mr Radcliffe, the new management team believed:

> The culture and climate of the new company will be created, not through corporate propaganda about values and behaviours, but through people's participation in the integration effort.

The senior management team decided to devolve much of the task of integration to those responsible at a regional or national level. This approach would obviously be more difficult to control and more risky, but the company felt the potential benefits outweighed the risks. Mr Radcliffe explains:

> The last thing we wanted was for our employees to turn around and say "well we never agreed to these changes" when, not if, the merger encountered problems further down the road. We wanted our managers to feel that they had driven the integration process and that it was their job to fix any problems that might arise.

UDV's integration got under way in January 1998. The company set up a steering committee made up of directors from UD and IDV. They worked on the overall strategy for the new business and set success factors for the integration process. These included "hard numbers" for growth targets and cost savings, and the timescales for delivering them. "Soft" success factors were encapsulated in *The UDV way of working*, a document that outlined the desired goals, culture, values and behaviours of the new business. Mr Radcliffe comments:

We set some fairly audacious goals – we wanted to challenge people and make everyone realise that we could not achieve these goals without new thinking.

A central but small integration programme office was established. Fewer than ten people worked in it, all selected on the basis of their skill in change management and project management, their knowledge of the business and their ability to "fashion structure out of chaos", says Mr Radcliffe. The office oversaw the activities of 11 "work streams" in procurement, sales and marketing, finance and administration, human resources and IT systems. Staffed by regional and functional representatives, these work streams had the task of eliminating duplication, achieving cost savings and establishing the basis for high levels of growth. A full-time communication team was created to help co-ordinate the flow of information to the market teams.

Human resources also played an important role in the merger. Stephen Dando, who was management development director at Diageo, believes that the appointment process for the new managing directors of the 50 or so market teams was particularly successful and helped reduce internal politics. He comments:

The period of waiting for regulatory clearance proved a very positive time to get the appointment process designed and agreed. After working intensively for two months, we came to the clear-headed decision that the MD appointments would be completely merit driven. There would be no score-keeping of "one for you, one for me". We were determined that we would do the best possible job in identifying the best individual for the job. We viewed appointments as an invaluable opportunity to improve the "gene pool" of the new organisation.

The bulk of integration was devolved to UDV's regional market teams during the six months from January to June 1998. The role of the centre was to equip the teams to handle this complex task. Each team was given an integration framework, a set of business goals and timescale for delivery, and a set of dates on which progress would be reviewed with senior managers. The general managers who headed these market teams were given considerable freedom to manage the task and could decide for themselves whether to make use of the tools and advice offered by the central integration team.

The integration framework developed by the central integration team was designed and packaged with a modular management approach, with much work done in workshops. Hundreds of employees attended workshops on such topics as "The UDV way of working" (including the company's integration philosophy), strategic planning, change management, decision-making and facilitating skills. Also covered were matters more specific to the business front line such as route to markets, supply chain guidelines, managing joint ventures and third-party arrangements, and brand management. The workshops sought to disseminate best practice and help employees to recognise the skills and expertise that already existed within their teams.

The most important aid to the market teams was the "integration road map", which provided a series of building blocks for the teams to work on. One section of the road map examined the process of designing a new organisational structure, highlighting two or three different models. Another part suggested a project-management process, with built-in "stop and think" review points. The aim of these reviews was to help the teams take time out to examine their own thinking and to judge whether they had genuinely looked for fresh solutions or simply chosen the most obvious or familiar process or structure. Another section provided a template for the teams to construct an integration plan for their part of the business, helping them to define their own goals, priorities, tasks and timescales.

The "stop and think" review stages provided useful learning opportunities, says Mr Radcliffe:

> We asked the teams to reach a point where they had a set of issues that they wanted to work through. A senior manager attended the review and held an open discussion and debate on the issues. It was their job to roll up their sleeves and offer practical help. We found that this provided valuable insights to the new management team and the central integration team. These reviews also became effective coaching sessions for the market teams. The whole process helped ensure that our integration process was aligned to UDV's business needs and emerging new culture.

At some point, all the various integration projects had to be pulled together to form a coherent view of a company-wide integration plan. This occurred in July 1998 when the management team took all the market teams' integration plans and added together the figures. According to Mr Radcliffe, the sum of the parts did not add up to the "audacious" whole that the UDV directors had hoped for. He explains:

> We knew there was a danger that the plans from the markets would not add up to the overall growth that we wanted. It became obvious that we needed to go for a radical solution.

The radical solution was to give priority to global brands by regrouping the market teams in three tiers. The most investment and support would be channelled into the top tier, made up of global brands within the best-performing markets – America, the UK, Ireland and Spain – which accounted for over half of Diageo's profits. Some of the market teams in this tier were accordingly asked to aim for more ambitious growth targets of around 10%, but they were also reassured that they would receive as much support as possible to achieve these targets. The second tier consisted of 15 "key" markets, which accounted for 25% of Diageo's profits but had the potential to become major markets. The third tier, "venture markets", made up the rest of Diageo's profits and were earmarked for more limited investment. Mr Radcliffe says:

> We were concerned that these teams would feel marginalised, but we gave the hard message that even though we would divert resources to the major markets, we still expected them to achieve their targets.

These changes were robustly discussed during a management conference in September 1998. Rather than derailing the integration, Mr Radcliffe believes:

> [The event] helped force out issues at an early rather than a later stage. The organisation was still fluid from the merger, and although the reviewed strategy meant some difficult decisions had to made about resources, our managers picked up the challenge and we addressed the issues as a whole company.

Diageo managers believe that the decentralised integration process worked well and helped build a groundswell of support for the merger, which has proved a positive foundation for the more recent merger of UDV and Guinness. Thousands of employees participated in the integration process, and Mr Radcliffe believes that even the employees who eventually lost their jobs were positive about the experience:

> People felt that they learnt a lot, that they were trusted and given useful tools. Many people went the extra yard because they wanted the integration to succeed. A good number of the people who lost their jobs saw their involvement as a positive means to sell themselves to a new employer. Ultimately, everyone knew that the new strategy was a winner.

Reaching an agreed definition of integration is crucial, and senior managers of the combining businesses should do this before detailed planning gets under way. The vision must be communicated to integration teams, whose members should have the opportunity to debate and refine what it means for them personally and for the business as a whole. They must also explore how the integration vision should influence their priorities and the way they achieve their specific project objectives. Another approach is for them to discuss how their attitudes, behaviours and actions could undermine the integration vision and create cynicism or suspicion among employees and other stakeholders, such as suppliers, customers and alliance partners.

It is only through such dialogue that leaders of the combining businesses have a chance of ensuring that their integration process will itself be a catalyst of change and be built around the desired behaviours, working practices, attitudes and values of the emerging new business.

A direct outcome should be that teams have a clear sense of their roles and remits. "Road maps" should be constructed in the following areas.

- An overview of their general role during integration, perhaps as change agents, cultural ambassadors, "transformers" or mobilisers – any phrase that encapsulates the integration vision. The global integration team at PricewaterhouseCoopers was clear about its role, as David Hadfield, the partner who headed the team, explains:

  When you are dealing with such a large merger between two partnerships, you cannot dictate or orchestrate the merger from the centre; you have to devolve it to the businesses as quickly as possible. Our role was to facilitate change and to point people in new directions. We also monitored progress by keeping an eye on whether different parts of the business were achieving their merger objectives and financial goals, especially in terms of controlling costs and attaining revenues.

- The remit of specific projects. For example:
  - What is the appropriate balance between establishing common standards and practices and encouraging diversity?
  - When should the team aim simply to improve, redesign, or achieve a step change?
  - What sort of balance should be struck between leading and facilitating?

- Should the teams take decisions, make recommendations or generate options?
- Should the teams direct other employees or teams in the operational business, or should they encourage them to take the lead?
- How much consultation and fact gathering is appropriate, given the time constraints of the project?
- Are they aiming to implement one particular approach or process, adopt the "best of both", or seek completely fresh approaches and solutions?

◪ Tracking combination synergies through specific projects, with an overlay of appropriate behaviours and practices that will help deliver these synergies during integration. Many companies already do the first task, but few link them to organisational and individual behaviour.

Taking the earlier example of Lloyds TSB adopting Scottish Widows's software, a road map should, as well as targets and timescales, include regular meetings that line managers should hold with their staff to discuss concerns and issues, such as whether and how these changes would affect people's career prospects. A checklist of appropriate behaviour (such as listening and asking open-ended questions) would give useful pointers about how to encourage staff to express their real views. If innovation were a desired synergy, the road map would include opportunities for employees to discuss the pros and cons of each other's IT processes and to identify opportunities for pooling their different expertise to create a new generation of software at some future point.

◪ A clear delineation of responsibility between different integration teams to minimise the possibility of friction or unhelpful competitiveness. This should include clear guidelines about the degree of information sharing and joint working. Teams should also be informed about the process for resolving any overlaps in activity or responsibility.

◪ A checklist of desirable behaviours and practices that help ensure all the integration teams behave consistently, in their dealings with both other teams and individual employees. In one company, for example,[3] the members of a joint operations task-force agreed to the following ground rules:
- try to reach a consensus, if possible, before convening a meeting;

- speak up during a meeting, rather than in outside hallways, if you do not agree with anything said;
- "respect" task-force meetings by arriving on time, or notifying people of your late arrival or absence;
- come to the meeting prepared;
- test emerging decisions with staff in your own work areas.

These may seem to reflect the kinds of business common sense and good manners that should be taken for granted, but with something as important as a merger it is always helpful to remind people of some of the basics.

Create a clear line of accountability, starting from the highest level

In successful M&As, the following managerial structure is often used.

- At the most senior level, a managerial committee oversees the whole integration process. This committee is usually made up of board members from both combining organisations and, when appropriate, representatives from the parent/group company. It should ideally include a director responsible for human resources or organisational development who will have enough insight and credibility to ensure that people-based issues receive high priority. In many cases, one director takes the role of championing the combination – in the case of genuine mergers, this role is often performed by two individuals, typically the CEOs of both companies. The committee sets the timetable for the integration programme, defines and agrees performance measures for the combining business during integration as well as integration performance measurements, specific targets, milestones and accountabilities. The committee takes decisions about important issues. It resolves problems, especially conflicts of interest between different groups of employees or business divisions (see next page).
- An integration manager – a senior manager who has responsibility for the integration programme.
- A core integration team – often around ten employees drawn from a variety of functions and specialisms – that helps co-ordinate various integration teams and track progress.
- Task-forces or integration teams responsible for specific projects.
- Project teams and other types of teams, looking at small, short-term projects or specific issues.

From co-ordination to change management

Montreal-based Abitibi-Consolidated, one of the world's largest producers of newsprint, used its merger steering committee, staffed by senior managers, to provide strategic direction in the early stage of the transition and then to promote organisational change as integration took place.[4]

In the first stage, the steering committee took a project-management-based approach by concentrating on defining and co-ordinating the integration activities. It defined the goals of the new organisation, its operating principles and desired end state. Working from these parameters, the committee formulated the critical success factors for the merger and used them to evaluate the various plans and recommendations made by the integration task-forces.

The steering committee also paid attention to the integration process, not just to project outputs. It issued integration task-forces with guidelines on how they should make recommendations about people, structures and processes and clarified the criteria that the committee would apply to these recommendations.

As the task-forces swung into action, Abitibi's steering committee shifted its attention towards ensuring that the integration activities resulted in real change. It worked hard to ensure that each action was understood within the context of a coherent change plan, helping task-forces to prioritise their activities. The steering committee also examined the likely impact of change, and particularly tried to tackle situations where changes were being implemented in a way that conflicted with the new operating principles. The managers of the steering committee sought to be role models of collaborative working and looked for opportunities to promote and support necessary changes in behaviour and mindsets.

Integration is a time-consuming and highly complex process, and it must be supported by a dedicated team that can respond immediately to problems and issues that arise. Even when the M&A is fairly small, it is desirable for the core integration team to be full-time. Experienced integrators such as GE Capital stress that operational managers become stretched when they have to manage integration and keep their own businesses on track.

Build appropriate integration performance measurements

Research by The Conference Board reveals that financial measures "dominate" performance measurement in M&As (see Chart 5.3).[5] The top

Chart 5.3 **Performance measures used most frequently to track M&A progress**

Measure	%
Operating income	92
Cost savings	92
Revenue	83
Head-count reduction	81
Market share	79
Speed of integration	78
Customer retention	72
IT systems integration	70
Product portfolio	66
Employee retention	64

Source: *Performance measurement during merger and acquisition integration*, The Conference Board, 2000

three most used performance measures are financial, and the last five relate to the integration process. The measure at the bottom of the list is employee retention. Given this list, it is hardly surprising that so many M&As fail to succeed because of people-related problems. If you are serious about making people-based changes, you must measure your performance in that area.

The same study also revealed that 57% of companies reported that their finance people were in charge of measuring the performance of an M&A integration, compared with 20% that said it was the integration manager or team and 13% that said it was operating managers. Interviews with survey respondents revealed that the dominance of financial specialists caused a number of problems.

- They often tracked what they were accustomed to.
- They did not set business process targets and measures.
- Financial measures and controls sometimes overwhelmed the measurement process.
- Softer people-based issues were not tracked.

An integration process must of course be designed around specific business and financial objectives that will help deliver the desired synergies of the combination. However, the role of people in delivering these benefits must be part and parcel of any performance measurement system. Only then can companies ensure that financial and business goals are not achieved at the expense of other important goals such as collaboration, employee retention and engagement and organisational learning.

The Conference Board highlights a number of examples in which companies are broadening their performance measures to include people-based measures. For example:

- Lucent's measures for M&A integration are employee retention, employee satisfaction, customer retention, and growth and speed of integration.

- At Science Applications International Corporation (SAIC), senior managers used a balanced scorecard during integration that included traditional metrics, such as revenue and sales, but also included retaining talent and low resignation rates.

- BP Amoco and Eastman Kodak placed great importance on managerial retention.

- Employee retention is of critical importance to Oracle, because of its practice of acquiring small high-technology companies and retaining the existing workforce.

- Lucent, BP Amoco and Abbott Laboratories use the measurement of employee satisfaction. They track this through a mixture of surveys and more qualitative approaches such as focus groups. Lucent decided to create a more formal process. In its recent acquisitions, the company has used either surveys or focus groups to gather employees' views about the clarity of strategy, the speed of execution and the clarity of their post-acquisition role. When Lucent reviews the success of its acquisitions, one of the four areas examined relates to "employee engagement and satisfaction".

- GE Capital measures cultural integration in a four-step process using cultural survey measurement data, such as focus groups, interviews, customer surveys and a "cultural workout" session between GE Capital and the acquired management team. The data are analysed to identify cultural similarities and differences. During the workout session, managers hold in-depth discussions about the nature of these differences and how they affect doing business. They formulate concrete plans for managing cultural issues and graft these on to the integration plan over the next 6–12 months.

Other performance measures could include organisational learning and knowledge sharing, or innovative capability. Once these measures are in place, they will give legitimacy to integration activities and processes that are aimed at encouraging employees to become involved with and support integration changes. Integration teams can then work with senior managers to define the types of people-based changes that are needed, not only to deliver financial and business synergies, but also to build a more collaborative organisation. Desired new working practices and behaviours must be clearly articulated and a set of objectives designed, with appropriate critical success factors or milestones (whatever project-management approach is used by the business) to help ensure that progress is achieved. As well as tangible "outputs", such as speeding up product development cycles, less tangible "inputs" could also be factored in, such as increasing joint working, sharing information and best practice, forging new internal linkages between different functions and divisions or finding ways to gather insights from customers, suppliers or alliance partners. If these people-related changes remain nebulous, they will be overshadowed by the pressure to deliver more tangible integration goals.

Make the integration team the nucleus of the new business

As this chapter has stressed, business combinations must begin to add value through synergies as soon as the deal is done. This task cannot be postponed until after the integration programme. In order to hit the ground running, the individuals and teams spearheading integration must become the nucleus of the emerging new business. Their challenge is to operate in such a way that they become the "positively charged" centre of the organisation around which other employees orbit, and the "base structure" for the new business. Just as in nuclear fusion, the process of creating a new nucleus from two combining nuclei involves huge amounts of energy. Integration teams must therefore be staffed with forceful and creative individuals who can create waves of change around them.

Role of the integration sponsor or champion

Ideally, the integration champion should be an executive who was involved with the M&A courtship. This helps ensure that there is strategic continuity as well as continued emphasis on the relationship between the combining businesses. The role of the champion is crucial, and whoever takes it on must:

◾ understand business strategy and have a detailed knowledge of how the two businesses operate. An understanding of the cultural make-up of the combining businesses, along with the ability to articulate people issues, is equally essential. All this should add up to an instinctual feel for the personality, "hearts and minds" of the combining organisations;

◪ understand the learning intent of the combination to help integration teams identify and leverage critical knowledge and capabilities among employees;

◪ ensure that the integration programme is adequately supported and resourced;

◪ demonstrate commitment to the combination and provide vision and direction. This is especially important when the going gets tough and unforeseen obstacles are encountered, or important targets and timescales are missed. To ensure success, the champion and sponsor must be willing to put his or her credibility on the line;

◪ set the tone for the new business, strongly emphasising the idea of mutual respect between the two organisations, even when one has been acquired by the other;

◪ act as a role model for the desired new behaviours and values;

◪ be politically adept, especially when "turf battles" flare up between different groups or divisions, or when an integration decision causes bitter division among employees;

Role of the integration manager

The integration manager has a highly complex role and must juggle many responsibilities and priorities (see "Integration 'gatekeepers' at GE Capital"). The role entails operating at many different levels and dealing with complex strategic as well as financial and operational issues. The ability to inspire staff, yet also liaise with the senior management board, is essential. The integration manager must:

◪ have strong project-management skills to keep track of the numerous projects running in tandem;

◪ be an effective communicator, recognising the importance of communicating frequently to stakeholders, especially employees and customers. Part of this task is to explain the potential benefits of the combination to all the stakeholders and to build support for the changeover;

◪ be adept at handling organisational and individual relationships, showing tact and diplomacy as different groups (especially the acquired management team) readjust their expectations or look for guidance and clarification about their new partners – by asking "stupid questions", as GE Capital says:

> People in a newly acquired company need someone they can talk to freely, to ask "stupid" questions, find out how things work at GE Capital and discover what resources are available and how to use them. They need a guide to the new culture and a bridge between their company and GE Capital.[6]

- have the skills to defuse political infighting and discourage political manoeuvrings, especially among middle and senior managers;
- build trust by being impartial and giving equal value and consideration to the views and expertise of both combining organisations;
- encourage mutual learning through the sharing of information and ideas and have the ability to turn failure into a positive learning experience. Employees need to be encouraged to take risks by sharing their ideas on how to achieve synergies and make improvements, or even dramatic step changes;
- have personal credibility and authority, and strong interpersonal and networking skills. These traits can play a crucial role in breaking down suspicion and fear among employees. When formal processes have broken down, an adept integration manager can play the role of diplomat and re-establish links between integration teams and disenfranchised groups of employees.

Integration "gatekeepers" at GE Capital

GE Capital views the integration manager's role as the "gatekeeper" of the emerging relationship between GE Capital and the acquired business. Two types of people are typically selected for the role. The first is "usually a less seasoned person with strong functional credentials who is viewed as a future business leader". This manager would normally oversee the acquisition of a small, straightforward or highly structured integration. The second is an experienced person with proven management skills who would be assigned to more complex acquisitions, especially those that combine multiple businesses. Both types of manager would have strong interpersonal skills and cultural sensitivity.

The role of integration managers has three dimensions.

1 Manage integration
- ◪ Work closely with the acquired management to make their practices consistent with GE Capital's specifications and standards.
- ◪ Formulate a communication plan for employees.
- ◪ Help the acquired business incorporate expertise and new functions such as risk management.

2 Help the acquired company understand GE Capital
- ◪ Help managers navigate through GE Capital's internal systems, such as the purchasing network.
- ◪ Coach managers about their owner's business cycle and business reviews, and other processes such as strategic planning and budgeting.
- ◪ Help managers understand GE Capital's culture and business customs.
- ◪ Help managers understand how the nature and scale of their roles have changed now that they are no longer heading an independent company.

3 Help GE Capital understand the acquired business
- ◪ Ensure that GE Capital does not swamp the newly acquired management team with requests for information so that they can stay focused on running the business during integration.
- ◪ Brief GE managers about the acquisition and explain why it works the way it does.

The core integration team

Members of the due diligence team should always be included in the core integration team as they should (in theory) have gained a deep knowledge of the acquired company or merger partner. They may have a detailed knowledge of potential barriers to engagement, and hopefully they will be some way down the road in their understanding of how the combined company can deliver synergies. Due diligence teams, especially functional specialists and operational managers, often return to their jobs after the transaction is completed. In the case of serial acquirers, they may form part of a dedicated resource and simply move on to the next deal. This can represent a serious loss of learning, and it is worth considering earmarking one individual to remain on the M&A team to ensure that the insights of the other members of the due diligence team are documented in some form and fed into the integration programme.

Representatives from all the combining organisations should be included in the integration process as soon as possible (in some cases, there are legal restrictions about when staff in a target company can be drawn in). Indeed, PA Consulting's survey[7] discovered that the inclusion of the acquired company's staff in the integration team "significantly improves the chances of extracting the target value" of a merger or acquisition.

Each set of representatives should have equal status in the teams, and senior management must repeatedly endorse this principle. Where a much larger and more financially successful business acquires a smaller player, it is common for the managers of the bigger business to assume that they possess superior expertise and have the natural right to lead the integration effort. Unless these assumptions are dispelled, those involved in engineering the integration process will quickly split into "them and us" factions, working against rather than with each other.

Those drawn from the combining organisations should not be merely "tokens", but should have the following qualities.

- Familiarity with their own organisation and understanding of its operational and cultural traits.
- Clearly recognisable personal abilities. Selecting someone simply because they fill a senior role is not sufficient. Individuals cannot afford to rely on their "ascribed" status in situations where a new organisation is emerging and where the normal mechanisms for ensuring the legitimacy of such status are no longer functioning. They need to be willing to "earn" their status by quickly engendering respect and credibility.
- Personal standing in their own organisation and an ability to network. This will reassure colleagues that they will wave the flag for and create a favourable perception of their "side". Employees also feel more positive about change when it is championed by people they trust and respect.

It is also helpful to include in the integration team employees from the acquiring company who joined the company through a merger or acquisition, and whose experience and ability to empathise with people will be valuable. Cisco Systems, a global provider of Internet networks, estimates that it has a pool of over 4,000 employees that can be seconded to the company's dedicated integration team. Their task is to help newcomers to "assimilate". Mimi Gigoux, head of the integration team, joined Cisco through its acquisition of Kalpana in 1994.

In an ideal world, members of the core integration team should have many of the skills and qualities of the team manager, notably:

- the ability to move easily between different roles;
- a strategic understanding and sound grasp of operational detail;
- strong project-management skills;
- interpersonal skills – especially tact, diplomacy, political sensitivity and cross-cultural awareness;
- personal credibility – the ability to command respect, to be viewed as objective (no personal agenda, not a "merger tsar");
- the ability to encourage and facilitate sharing of ideas – knowledge sharing requires building trust too;
- creativity and pragmatism – the ability to question the unquestionable or the taken for granted and recognise opportunities for improvement or complete step change, mixed with a realistic sense of what can be achieved in the time span and in accordance with the capacity of the merging organisation's ability to change.

Lift-off, maintenance and repair

For integration teams to function effectively, Mitchell Lee Marks and Philip Mirvis, two M&A experts, emphasise the need to "attend to the team's internal processes". They argue that like any start-up group, integration teams, or "transition task-forces", go through stages of "forming, storming and norming". They advise:

> Task-force leaders and members are well advised to stay on top of the group dynamics influencing their deliberations and devote some time to group development and maintenance. Members of task-forces need to maintain a sense of humour and get to know each other as people as well as professionals.

In one organisation, they point out, "internal facilitators were trained to assist each transition team and work with team leaders to ensure positive and productive relations among team leaders".

They also recommend nurturing the integration teams' relationships with the rest of the organisation. These teams should not appear to be competing against operational managers or dictating how the organisation should go about its business. They should "facilitate the work of others" and "respect normal decision-making channels in the enterprise". However, because of their unfixed position in the core business, Messrs Marks and Mirvis argue that it is essential that senior managers give their support and commitment to the work of these teams.

They have used a formal two-day launch meeting for transition teams to help them "form, storm and norm". During this period, the teams review the rationale, vision, critical success factors and operating principles of the combination. They discuss their "charter", or role and remit, responsibilities, deliverables and timetable. They are also led through the potential pitfalls of group decision-making and learn how to conduct "creative problem analysis". Trained facilitators work with the teams to develop "ground rules". They look at the way they want to function as a team – for example, how they would prefer to make decisions and interact with each other. All the teams discuss areas of ambiguity and overlap and clarify which teams own various functions during the transition. Messrs Marks and Mirvis claim:

> *Without some developmental kick-off like a launch meeting, task-forces usually take several weeks or a few months to make this much progress."*

Speed counts

After holding brief talks, Price Waterhouse and Coopers & Lybrand announced in September 1997 their intention to merge their accountancy and consultancy businesses. The merger promised to be highly complex, given the need to gain approval from each firm's partnerships in 150 countries as well as clearance from regulators in America and the EU. The merged business would have approximately 146,000 employees and an annual revenue of $15 billion in its first year.

To gain the approval of the two firms' partners, the merger team, composed of approximately 20 senior partners from both firms, circulated a merger prospectus outlining the benefits of the merger, the new business strategy and an outline organisation structure. Following a secret ballot in November 1997, both partnerships approved the merger.

The first step was to appoint a global leadership team for the new business, a process that "inevitably involved politics and a degree of horse trading in order to achieve some sort of balance of power between the two firms", says Ed Smith, who is responsible for global education and learning at PricewaterhouseCoopers (PWC). The team, identified in January 1998, concentrated on defining various global product lines and agreeing their scope and performance objectives. The team members also began discussing how they could ensure that the knowledge and expertise of both firms could be combined into "best of both" processes and products.

The global integration team was also selected in January 1998 and headed by David Hadfield. Senior managers decided to keep the central integration team as small as possible, around a dozen people, with the aim of devolving integration to the business units as quickly as possible. Mr Hadfield's team worked closely with the global management team to develop a set of "value drivers" for the integration process. These included ensuring revenue growth; finding ways to "energise people and keep them on board and excited"; staying focused and in control of the business partnership; constantly communicating to employees and the marketplace; and controlling costs. A communications strategy was designed in line with these values, which included at one point weekly newsletters to employees and a regular random survey of 200 employees that acted as a "spot check" on how well they understood various aspects of the merger integration.

A "high-level" organisational structure was also designed, based on a matrix structure that proved difficult to implement. Both firms were historically based on geography, which meant that the practices in the various countries largely determined how they would operate. PWC's new global management team wanted to create a global partnership, so they tried to regroup activities around industry sector (for example, financial services), line of service (such as auditing, tax advice and management consultancy) and geography (national countries).

In the event, a power struggle developed between the newly appointed senior managers responsible for line of service and the existing heads of the regional practices. PWC is still trying to improve the matrix structure, mainly by encouraging middle and senior managers to focus first and foremost on client needs.

By May 1998, regulators in both America and Europe had cleared the merger, and it was legally completed in June 1998. PWC then set itself the ambitious target of bolting together the two firms by July 1999. In fact, the global integration team achieved its targets before schedule and was disbanded in May 1999. Much of the integration process focused on standardising critical processes, especially auditing methods.

Mr Smith comments:

> We had no choice but to bang together our auditing processes as quickly as possible and to train 65,000 employees in the new methodology by December 1998. Inevitably, people had built up an expertise in their own methodology and had a vested interest in its continued use. But in fact, people gave their intellectual buy-in to the new methodology very quickly, and the emotional buy-in quickly followed. The most valuable outcome was that it required everyone to work together and make compromises in

order to get the whole thing working, and this helped speed the process of cultural integration between the two firms.

Integrating various support processes such as human resources and financial systems was a more lengthy and complex task than expected. Indeed, the "nuts and bolts" of integration can become overwhelming in large mergers, prompting Mr Hadfield's advice not to underestimate how much strain is placed on a company's "infrastructure" and to also keep a strict eye on merger costs.

Achieving cultural integration between two firms that were once rivals is seen as a continuing task and not something that can be achieved through "training sessions and 'love-ins'", says Mr Smith. One solution is to keep people focused on delivering a higher-quality, global service to clients. Another is to use every means – some technology-based, some involving encouraging informal networking – to get employees to share their knowledge and expertise.

Ultimately, cultural integration depends on middle and senior managers adopting new behaviours and being willing to collaborate with former rivals. Mr Smith comments:

Successful integration is about managers being willing to mix their teams in order to find the best combination of experience and expertise. It's about how we do business, how we form teams, how managers interact with their people on a daily basis. Getting it right at that level is the only way that we will build a stronger business.

This chapter has focused on the need to view integration as a collaborative process that helps integration teams become the "positively charged" centre of the emerging business. Any integration process must seek to engage as many employees as possible from the first day of the new combination. However, when considering the diverse approaches that can be adopted, the advice that GE Capital gives to its integration managers when using the company's Pathfinder model probably says it all:

The model's neat and systematic appearance belies the fact that acquisition integration is as much art as science ... but there are aspects of every acquisition/integration that are new or unique. As in any major organisational transformation, managers will have to improvise.

6 Explosions and implosions: the Achilles heel between announcement and closure

THE MERGER ANNOUNCEMENT and run-up to the legal closure is a crucial period in the process of getting employees and other stakeholders to endorse the logic and merit of the new venture and to invest their skills and energies into making it succeed. An M&A announcement sends shock waves of uncertainty through the organisations involved. These need to be responded to immediately, not after the deal has gone through. The organisations' intellectual and emotional assets must be protected, and so a climate should be created in which employees, apprehensive as they are, are able and prepared to think about their future and that of their organisation in a new way.

Communication is the "safety pin" helping to create linkages between the still separate businesses during the waiting period between the announcement of the deal and the legal completion. Communication is the only way to fill the void between what is planned and when it can be implemented, a void that can grow alarmingly if closure of the deal is delayed. Into that void can disappear positive messages, reassurances, promises and visions of a more successful future. Out of the void can come fear, rumours, anger and distrust. All the hard work of the courtship can be wasted if there is a failure to provide leadership and direction.

It is a mistake to assume that integration cannot begin before the legal closure and that until then communication processes can do little other than reassure employees. The truth is that a lot can be done before closure to create the climate that will encourage people to work together successfully and therefore can lay the foundation on which the new business is built. It is often assumed that pre-acquisition collaboration is something that happens only between the top teams during the M&A courtship and that collaborative working among the wider workforce is a post-acquisition activity. In the most extreme cases, some go so far as to view collaboration as a post-integration event, something that will somehow magically happen once the dust has settled and those working on the integration programme have returned to their former roles.

Nigel Slater, a merger consultant at Andersen, an international accounting and consulting firm, describes this attitude. He says:

> Many companies select Churchill-style "war leaders" who utilise a combination of personal charisma, decisiveness and ruthlessness to drive the merger programme forward. Once the process has been completed, they then opt for a change of emphasis towards "healing the wounds" and redefining a new, more collegiate corporate style to cement the new partners' formerly competing cultures.

Collaboration will not spring mushroom-like out of a merger. It must be striven for at every level and become an integral part of how employees think and act – in short, part of the fabric of the merging new business. It is definitely a pre-acquisition issue – something that must be considered from the day of the merger announcement. Communication is at the heart of successful collaboration (see Chart 6.1 on the next page), and its use must be intelligently planned.

Communication sets the tone for what is happening both in the message and the way the message is put across. It reflects the professionalism (or not) of the new management team, its style, values and attitudes to the various stakeholders.

For example, staff at Texas, a DIY business, were unanimously unimpressed with the way managers at Homebase, the DIY subsidiary of J. Sainsbury, a British retailer, handled the announcement of the acquisition. They were used to colourful presentations from their own managers, often involving state-of-the-art technology. Messages were sent via satellite television to every Texas outlet or office so that the whole company would be informed at the same time. Senior managers at Homebase instead did what they thought mattered: face-to-face presentations and exhausting "road shows" at Texas sites. This direct form of communication was either badly done or misjudged, as Texas people saw it as a dull and even patronising. A Texas marketing manager admits:

> Many of us were hostile during Homebase's presentation about the acquisition. We had a very confrontational question-and-answer session afterwards. The managers were unprepared for this reaction and did not handle the discussions very well.

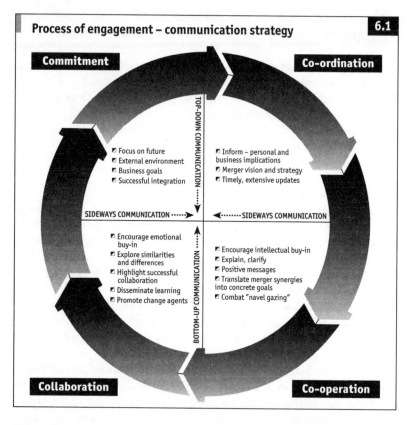

Process of engagement – communication strategy `6.1`

(Diagram content: Commitment — Focus on future, External environment, Business goals, Successful integration. Co-ordination — Inform – personal and business implications, Merger vision and strategy, Timely, extensive updates. Collaboration — Encourage emotional buy-in, Explore similarities and differences, Highlight successful collaboration, Disseminate learning, Promote change agents. Co-operation — Encourage intellectual buy-in, Explain, clarify, Positive messages, Translate merger synergies into concrete goals, Combat "navel gazing". Axes: TOP-DOWN COMMUNICATION, BOTTOM-UP COMMUNICATION, SIDEWAYS COMMUNICATION.)

Managing "announcement day": the medium is the message

In the announcement of an M&A, there must be intelligent co-ordination – both in what they say and how they are communicated – of the messages given to shareholders and analysts, employees, customers, suppliers and alliance partners. Whether they are face-to-face presentations, press releases, letters and videos or whatever, the most important task is to make clear the strategic rationale for the union, the objectives, the expected benefits (customised for each group) and the mission and value of the new business. If the company's name is to be changed, the rationale behind and advantages of the new name must be consistently and coherently explained.

The information and insights from the due diligence team should help determine the most appropriate way to make an M&A announcement to employees. Options could include the following.

Face-to-face presentations followed by question-and-answer sessions

This may be appropriate for smaller deals where it is possible to bring together all the members of an organisation in one location. It is most likely to be the best approach for organisations that value face-to-face communication and personal networking, or that have cultures that foster open discussion. But however successful face-to-face presentations appear to be, they must be followed up. It is often only after the event that questions occur to employees, and, in any case, many people lack the confidence to ask questions on such occasions, especially when senior managers are present.

Satellite TV and/or Internet broadcasts

This may be appropriate for companies that value these mediums. In larger M&AS, it may be the only practical way of ensuring that thousands of employees in dispersed locations receive the announcement at the same time.

E-mail

This may be effective in situations where news of the announcement is likely to leak out before senior managers address their organisations. Employees can read the e-mail and then attend a fuller presentation later in the day. Although an e-mail may seem impersonal, it can help prevent staff learning about the merger or acquisition through other channels, such as local radio, or from friends and associates outside the organisation. Mistimings in merger announcements can and do occur, especially in the case of public companies, because of the requirement that the deal is announced first to the financial markets. In the case of one financial services company, senior managers were presenting their merger to the City while TV camera crews set up outside the corporate headquarters to solicit the views of staff as they arrived for work. A manager comments:

> We were all ready to talk to our people, but our job was made much harder by the fact that by the time they arrived at work, many of them were very annoyed to have heard the news from the local media and on the radio.

Local management presentations

This may be appropriate for global companies where it is impossible to announce the link-up simultaneously, and for companies that prefer a more devolved structure or where decentralised communication is the norm. When Eastern Electricity, now part of TXU Energi, bought a number of well-performing power stations from a competitor, it was decided to let the power-station managers handle the announcement to their employees. Each power station had its own strong culture and relationships between staff and managers were good. Each station manager became a "buffer" between staff and the new owners, and all communications from the parent company were channelled through the station manager. Each manager was "deliberately made to appear to be in control of the station", says John Herbert, then the group's human-resources manager.

> We decided that local autonomy should be paramount and that the centre would simply impose some financial controls and then offer advice and pointers to good practice.

The NTL way

Managing a merger process is all the harder when there is a long gap between negotiating and completing the deal. NTL, a British cable telecommunications operator, had to wait almost a year before it received regulatory approval for its purchase of CWC, Cable & Wireless's consumer business. NTL used the time to construct a communications strategy that was designed around the way people typically react during a merger. NTL may have run into problems over its high level of debt, but the M&A principles and actions outlined below are instructive.

Phil Pavitt, NTL's director of integration, says that getting the best from people is more than "just logistics and processes". He explains:

> It is about heart and soul and engaging people. We realised early on how important communication would be, given the sheer weight of issues for our employees and the complexity of change involved.

Mr Pavitt and his team developed a set of principles for all forms of communication during the merger. Processes should:

- support NTL's brand values and business goals;
- support managers in their role as communicators;
- use informal processes and face-to-face communication to build relationships;
- provide opportunities for feedback and regularly monitor concerns among employees;

■ enable line managers to be the first to relay important changes to employees.

NTL's integration team worked with consultants from MCA BannerMcBride to design a three-phase communications programme based on the way people adjust to change. Jacqui Hitt, the consultant working with NTL, says:

> As we moved through each phase, the emphasis changed from sharing information to involving employees in creating the future. It was essential to ensure that everyone understood the big picture before they could get to grips with what it meant for them and what specific actions they needed to take.

Phase 1: preparing for "day one"
Based on straw-poll research into the concerns of employees, a weekly electronic bulletin and intranet site was launched to provide up-to-date information about the approaching merger and to answer questions and concerns.

Face-to-face communication was considered a priority, so NTL and CWC arranged meetings and social events for approximately 100 senior managers. "These were great levellers and ice-breakers," says Mr Pavitt. The week before the merger was completed, middle managers attended one-day briefings.

To encourage wider participation, NTL gathered together 100 employees with leadership and influencing skills. They were briefed about the merger and encouraged to act as a "positive virus" in supporting integration. Ms Hitt comments: "We showed them how to use their natural abilities to have a positive influence on their peers."

Phase 2: days 1–30 – going live
Up-to-the-minute communication was the priority, especially on the day that the merger was legally completed. Welcome letters from NTL's CEO were sent electronically to all CWC employees. A special bulletin was also sent to employees working in over 300 locations. NTL's brand values were communicated via a corporate video, integration puzzle and competition.

Over 100 briefings by senior managers from both NTL and CWC took place around the UK.

A merger bulletin, *Right here, right now*, was circulated weekly. Each issue sought to respond to the changing concerns among employees, judged through regular straw polls and conference calls with different groups of employees around the UK.

Phase 3: Days 30–90 – sustaining momentum
As well as providing accurate and frequent information, NTL prioritised the need to

support senior managers by providing regular update sessions and support packs.

Sustaining momentum is also about helping people to appreciate what the merger has already achieved. After the first two months, NTL updated everyone on progress using, among other things, a video highlighting merger achievements and a special edition of the merger bulletin.

As the organisation was restructured, supportive measures included workshops and telephone polls to help determine how employees were reacting to the changes, and what more could be done to help them adjust.

Mr Pavitt is positive about the value of the communication programme. He comments:

> When people talk about the successes of our integration, the lion's share is linked to the strength of our communication planning and delivery. We firmly believe that we have built a solid foundation for the new business to work from.

Consistent messages

"Announcement day" must be well planned. Senior managers will be briefed before the M&A announcement by human-resources and communication specialists. On the day of the announcement, the CEO or chairman will usually handle the M&A announcement, with senior managers filling in details where appropriate. Employees in the organisations involved may receive some form of "information" or "welcome" pack, containing items such as press releases, annual reports, a letter from the chairman, facts sheets, employee handbooks and perhaps a brief statement about how the merger is likely to affect pay and benefits. Senior managers then have responsibility for further meetings with their staff to discuss the change.

To engage employees both intellectually and emotionally, the following information should be given.

An explanation of the vision, logic and business benefits of the merger
This is especially important if the merger will:

- enable the company to move into new lines of business;
- create new linkages between different services and products;
- necessitate the disposal of healthy or high-performing business divisions or subsidiaries;

◪ cause job losses and/or relocation;
◪ involve combining with a major rival.

It is the job of managers to ensure that those that they manage understand and accept the business case for the M&A. Simply saying the business will be bigger is unlikely to motivate people or justify the uncertainty and disruption that many will experience over the following months. Ironically, gaining intellectual buy-in can be more difficult in the acquiring company than in the target business, as a Halifax Building Society (which became a bank and later merged with Bank of Scotland to form HBOS) manager explained:

> When we acquired the Leeds Building Society, we found that
> the Leeds people were well aware of the challenges of the
> external business environment and were relieved to be bought
> by us after some months of uncertainty. What we did not
> expect was the reaction of our own staff. Many felt that we
> were already highly successful and that the acquisition was an
> unnecessary source of disruption and additional work.

It is helpful to include a brief overview of the activities of the merger partner or acquisition and the reasons it was selected. A clear description of the complementary strengths of the organisations is also helpful. Focus groups with employees frequently reveal that people have preconceptions and prejudices about their potential partner that can impede collaboration after the merger – even more so in cross-border unions. In the case of M&As involving rivals, each business may have built up myths that portray the other in unhelpfully demonical terms. The fact is that whatever perceptions of its competitor's respective strengths and weaknesses a firm has, some of these views will be accurate, some will not, and some will not square with the rationale for the M&A.

For example, Halifax staff assumed that Leeds staff would be less professional.[1] The Leeds people appeared to act in ways that were "sloppy and informal", yet to the bewilderment of Halifax staff, their senior managers seemed to endorse their method of working. What Halifax's merger team had failed to do was to explain that one of the reasons for the acquisition was to benefit from the smaller firm's more entrepreneurial (and inherently informal) culture. It is important to correct or realign perceptions about the M&A partner from the outset.

Details of the new senior management team and an outline of how and when other management tiers will be selected

This requires careful handling because of emotional and political sensitivities about who has been retained, let go, moved sideways or moved down. Criticism or derogatory remarks about the target company's outgoing management team should be avoided as they may encourage employees to feel that they as well as their organisation are being belittled and patronised, which will make them more defensive or aggressive, thus stopping future collaboration in its tracks. Collaboration depends on mutual respect – an M&A announcement is the ideal time to acknowledge the strength and qualities of the other management team and the achievements of their business.

An overview of the integration process

This should include the expected timescale and likely new organisational structure, including decisions about site closures and redundancies or, if this is not yet clear, a timetable of when and how these decisions will be made. In some cases, there will have been time to prepare a detailed integration plan. In many cases, however, managers may have only a rudimentary plan. In such circumstances, they are often deeply uncomfortable about their inability to give details and answers, and when put on the spot are sometimes tempted to make rash promises. This is a mistake: breaking promises is the surest and best way to prevent trust from developing in a new organisation. It is much better to be open: to admit that parts of the integration plan are still being developed. Employees often assume that cataclysmic change will overcome them immediately, but the message from successful mergers is that people appreciate it when the integration timeframe is clearly explained and they can judge when different parts of the business are likely be affected.

Details of changes to employment terms and conditions or when the two companies' systems will be harmonised

Due diligence should have revealed the facts about pay and conditions and highlighted the potential problems of harmonisation. Where trade unions and employee councils have been closely involved during negotiations, the principles that will apply for the new business may already have been agreed upon. In complex mergers, however, it may take several months to harmonise conditions and require the help of remuneration specialists. This is even more likely in companies where large numbers of employees have negotiated their own remuneration packages. Even in fairly simple M&As, remuneration issues can become a flashpoint in the integration process. Although employees always ask for details on announcement day, some experienced acquirers simply provide some broad principles, such as reassurances that people will not lose out financially, or that employee share schemes will continue, or that there will be no lapse of medical or dental coverage. They then emphasise that employees will have the opportunity to hold detailed discussions at some point with line managers and human-resources staff.

Below is a description of how Cisco, a global provider of Internet networks, was handling announcement day during the heady days of the technology boom. Whether the well-oiled approach, greatly helped by sweeteners in the form of shares and promises of no job losses, can be sustained remains to be seen.

Cisco Systems: the "Borg" of our times?

Cisco's integration team have sometimes been dubbed "the Borg", a race of technologically obsessed half robots featuring in "Star Trek", who forcefully assimilate their victims within hours of their capture. Cisco is open to this quip because its transition approach has been perfected over a number of years in many fast-growing technology companies. Cisco's priority is to achieve a smooth transfer of employment so that the business continues to maintain its speed of growth and is not needlessly distracted by worrying about Cisco's intentions.

For several weeks before the announcement, the company's centralised, full-time integration team works hard to harmonise terms and conditions. For example, following its acquisition in 1999 of Cerent, a fibre-optics equipment maker, Cisco prepared detailed information for employees. John Chambers, CEO of Cisco, and Carl Russo, CEO of Cerent, personally addressed Cerent employees on the day of the announcement. During the next two days, they and other senior managers hosted follow-up question-and-answer sessions. A primary message was that there would be no job losses. To further reassure employees, many of whom came from the telephone-equipment industry and associated M&As with layoffs, Mr Chambers explained that, for once, Cisco had given Rosso the permanent right to veto any decisions about redundancies that Cisco might make in the future.

After the announcement, employees were handed a folder with information about Cisco, the phone numbers and e-mail addresses of seven Cisco executives, and an eight-page chart comparing the vacation, medical and retirement benefits of the two companies. They also received detailed information about the financial terms of the deal so that they could calculate how much their Cerent shares were worth. It was a pleasant surprise for many.

Source: *Wall Street Journal*, March 1st, 2000

Preparing and supporting managers

In dealing with employees, managers need to be aware that they are in effect ambassadors whose views, behaviours and attitudes are being scrutinised intensely. When an M&A is under way, the environment can be highly charged and highly political, and a careless or insensitive remark can instantly ripple through the organisation, setting off fresh waves of anxiety or resentment.

Patti Hanson, a human-resources and M&A specialist,[2] believes that the line managers (or facilitators, as she calls them) involved in announcement day have a vital role to play in helping the merger or acquisition succeed. She declares:

> They can set the tone for the transaction. Those selected are ideally the leaders who will serve in the new combined organisations. They must be able to share the vision of the future company, understand the reasons for and benefits of the merger, and positively deliver the message to employees who may doubt the rationale for the transaction. With the proper commitment and conviction, the facilitators will begin to instil the excitement and pride that is so critical during times of stress and uncertainty.

Managers who are not well prepared often "shoot from the hip", Ms Hanson points out. She advocates preparing them through training and coaching, and suggests that they should be given the following.

- A high-quality information pack – and enough time to familiarise themselves with the content. The pack should include instructions for the day, written scripts for less confident speakers, details about the communication process, communication documents, presentation materials, question-and-answer sheets and handouts.
- Training to allow them to practise their presentation and answer

questions. It is helpful if more senior managers, especially those involved at the start of the M&A, attend the session and supply direct answers "without interpretations and filters from others".

◪ In the case of managers in remote locations, coaching through conference calls, video teleconferences and Internet broadcasts.

◪ Useful advice about how to handle their staff, especially those that are likely to be upset or angry about the changeover. Ms Hanson suggests the following.

· Be willing to say "I don't know".
· Be willing to admit "it hasn't been decided yet".
· Talk to people directly and, if possible, in person.
· After meetings, write to anyone who could not attend and supply the same information.
· Speak the truth.
· Don't make promises that cannot be fulfilled.
· Acknowledge that unpleasant things might happen.
· Listen to employees' concerns and be tolerant of them.
· Renew the focus on the business goals of the M&A.

Few companies provide enough support to the senior managers of the acquired company, particularly when they will not be retained in the new business (see Janet Tapsell's experience below). This is a mistake as research reveals that those managers have a more profound influence on the attitudes of their employees than the leadership of the acquiring company. Gaining their commitment to the changeover may make all the difference in collaborative M&As.

M&A INSIGHTS

Janet Tapsell is the former human-resources director of Burmah Petroleum Fuels, a subsidiary of Burmah Castrol that was acquired by Save in 1995

"One day, I and my fellow directors were called into the room by a director from our parent company and told that our business was being sold and that it was our responsibility to keep the business running and to provide the necessary information for the due diligence process. Although we knew that the decision was intellectually completely correct, we were shocked. Everyone had worked incredibly hard for the last four years to turn the business around and we had succeeded in creating a united and focused organisation. However, we were being sold to what we felt, and what we thought our employees would feel, was more of a 'cut-price' petrol business, and it was very likely that under this type of business many of our people would be made redundant.

"None of our directors were involved in the sale negotiations. We found ourselves in a very difficult position during the due diligence process. It was onerous and made us very aware of our responsibilities as directors – we had to provide an enormous amount of information and also sign various warranties and guarantees. In an open, friendly company, we suddenly had to be very secretive and smuggle company data out late at night for the lawyers to look over before start of business the next morning.

"It was hard to run the business as usual during the four months prior to the completion of the sale, and to proceed with plans that we knew would never be implemented. Rumours were beginning to circulate and we felt very pressurised and uncomfortable when our people asked us direct questions. For example, I was asked directly whether an employee should sign a new mortgage or not.

"On the positive side, when we informed our employees about the sale when the contracts were signed, we were able to say that we had not been involved in the decision to sell and that we felt as they did. This helped minimise a feeling of 'them and us' during the time until completion and helped stabilise the situation. I was also able to convince Save's CEO to let me devise a communications plan for announcements day that would ensure that our employees were treated professionally, especially if they were to lose their jobs. This enabled us to handle things 'our way' and to ensure that employees received help, such as lists of local vacancies, as soon as we announced the sale.

"Burmah Castrol was very supportive and allowed me, with the agreement of Save, to transfer as many people as possible to jobs in BC. It also allowed me, during the due diligence period, to transfer across for six months and thus concentrate on the communications plan, knowing I could sort out my personal situation later. We were very open with our people about the likelihood of them losing their jobs, and although there were times when lawyers on both sides weren't happy about what we said, we felt strongly that we wanted to treat people with dignity and give them the opportunity to make their own decisions.

"I felt I learnt a number of useful lessons.

- It was right to manage the communications ourselves and to ensure that people heard the news from their own directors and then received practical help and advice immediately.
- Due diligence was made much easier by the fact that the directors had close working relationships with each other and were able to provide the due diligence team with a consistent and accurate picture of the business.

◪ My colleagues and I would have benefited from some practical help and training in how to field awkward questions.

◪ Being part of a supportive team was very valuable and helped us deal with the conflict between wanting to be open with our own people yet needing to fulfil our legal responsibilities.

◪ I learnt about myself – I discovered that I could work at a high level of pressure, both physical and emotional, and deliver complex, detailed and accurate work over a sustained period of time.

◪ It is sometimes necessary to follow your instincts and take the risk of telling lawyers to back off."

David Schweiger and Yaakov Weber, two academics who specialise in the study of M&As, interviewed 166 employees from acquired *Fortune* 500 companies.[3] They discovered that employees in the acquired business set greater store on the behaviours and actions of their managers (especially their immediate boss) than on the promises and actions of the acquiring managers. They also identified the following differences between effective and ineffective managers in acquired companies.

Commitment and companionship

◪ Effective managers get alongside their team and try to act as a friend. They try to protect their employees and provide a sense of security in the run-up to the acquisition.

◪ Ineffective managers become withdrawn and appear to abdicate responsibility for their teams. They seem preoccupied with self-preservation and their own career prospects.

Honesty and openness

◪ Effective managers are honest and do not make any false promises. They are as open as possible and pass on as much information as they can about approaching changes. They are willing to admit when they do not know something. This does not stop staff from leaving before the acquisition is completed, but employees feel more in control and equipped to make their own decisions.

◪ Ineffective managers sometimes lie or fail to keep their promises. This makes their staff more anxious and less committed to the business.

Understanding employee concerns

- Effective managers show concern for staff in simple ways, often by just listening to them. This helps employees feel valued.
- Ineffective managers show little understanding and employees find it more difficult to work through their anger and anxiety.

Minimising political behaviour

- Effective managers work hard to maintain a team atmosphere. They discourage destructive personal or political behaviour. When making staffing decisions, they use performance criteria that can be seen to be objective.
- Ineffective managers are biased towards their "favourites", causing rivalry and divisions among their staff.

Handling job losses

- When people have to be fired before the transfer of ownership, effective managers act as "a valuable buffer" between the organisation and those who are being made redundant, helping them through the experience. This helps remaining employees to feel more loyal to their company and more confident about how they will be treated after the acquisition.
- Ineffective managers do not demonstrate the same care, making it more likely that their staff feel disconnected and insecure about their future, and antagonistic towards their employer.

Preparing staff for the takeover

- Effective managers actively seek to reduce a sense of "them and us" between the acquired company and its future new owner. They try to obtain as much information as possible about the new owners. They contact their counterparts and work hard to ensure that their own staff will not see the other management team as "the bad guys".
- Ineffective managers do not do this, making it harder for their staff to begin the process of becoming "emotionally attached" to the other organisation.

In any acquisition, the new owners should make the most of the role that the managers of the acquired business can play after the announcement has been made by taking the following actions.

- Create opportunities to meet senior and middle managers to build a relationship between them and the acquiring company.
- Consider some form of mentoring or shadowing scheme – taking care that it does not appear patronising – to help inform those in the acquired company about processes that are likely to be changed, such as reporting procedures and financial planning.
- Create a tailored communications plan for the management team of the acquired company and aim to inform them as soon as possible of the likely impact of the combination on them personally.
- Communicate the goals and vision for the combination, and include any promises or undertakings that have been made during negotiations. Do not rely on the directors of the acquired company passing on this information accurately or promptly, especially if directors' own futures are under threat.
- Make it clear that past achievements, skills and experiences will be considered in the light of any decisions about appointments or redundancies. Emphasise that experience is still perceived as valuable even if the combined business is likely to be managed differently, for example, shifting from a regional basis to a product basis.
- Include managers who are highly regarded in the acquired business in integration teams and task-forces.

Between announcement and closure: the "Achilles heel"

Once the announcement has been made, the combining businesses can become unstable. Price Pritchett, chairman and CEO of Price Pritchett, an American consultancy specialising in organisational change, believes that this loss of stability has the potential to be either a problem or an opportunity. He declares:

> The organisation becomes jittery, off balance, destabilised.
> People are hyper-alert, maybe shaken out of their routines and
> primed for change. Interestingly, the destabilisation caused by
> a merger powerfully increases the energy level in a company.
> But unless that energy gets channelled along productive lines, it
> is a destructive force that can sabotage corporate effectiveness.

The destructive forces that Mr Pritchett describes appear in a number of guises. The period between the M&A announcement and the point of "closure", when contracts are signed and the legal transaction is completed, has been dubbed the "Achilles heel" of M&As. During this waiting period, the momentum built up during the courtship can become dissipated as the members of the merger team refocus on their own businesses, often realising that performance may have suffered from management inattention. The rumour mill swings into action at this time, making employees anxious.

- Valued staff leave. An M&A often results in large-scale job cuts, especially when the operations of the combining businesses overlap.
- Typically, headhunters and competitors exploit this time of uncertainty by propositioning valued staff. For example, during 2000, Paine Webber took legal action against Morgan Stanley, a major investment-banking rival, in an attempt to place a restraining order preventing it from poaching staff from Paine Webber's merger partner, Bradford. The company accused its rival of a "carefully planned, broad-based campaign to raid Bradford personnel and to interfere with the merger agreement between Paine Webber and Bradford".[4]
- Leaders of the acquired company feel directionless and retreat into "crisis management". Messrs Schweiger and Weber found in their survey of acquired companies that:

  Top management were so caught up in surviving the deal that not enough time and attention had been given to employee concerns. Even when employees were considered, managers faced so much uncertainty and ambiguity about the future that they were not always clear about what actions needed to be taken and by whom. Several top managers described their situation as requiring "crisis management skills" and taking actions incrementally. None felt that broad-based action or long-term plans could be laid.

- No news becomes bad news in people's minds if there is little communication while the legalities of the combination are being finalised. Silences in M&As become destructive – in the absence of information, employees resort to the informal grapevine. Unless there is a constant drip of information, speculation and misinformation will take over. Any positive responses there have been to the initial announcement may dissipate as employees become increasingly anxious about their future.

◪ There are big increases in workload. An M&A announcement will trigger a series of reactions among suppliers, customers and alliance partners, all of whom are likely to besiege the employees they deal with requests for further information, clarification, reassurance, and so on (see below.)

Bristol & West: besieged by "carpetbaggers"

The legal intricacies of being bought by Bank of Ireland and relinquishing its mutual status meant that the transfer of ownership of UK-based Bristol & West Building Society took 16 months. This interim period placed B&W under enormous strain. At a time when financial services firms within the UK were undergoing rapid consolidation, B&W was left in limbo, unable to move forward until the legal change of ownership was completed. According to Kevin Flanagan, then human-resources director, he and his colleagues were intensely aware that "the world outside was changing quickly, yet we were forced to mark time. It was basically a year out of our lives".

B&W employees were almost overwhelmed by the workload generated by the changeover. Scenting the likelihood of a deal and a payout on demutualisation, "carpetbaggers" had flocked to B&W, resulting in 160,000 new accounts. Membership records had to be updated in time for the Special General Meeting where members would vote on the proposed sale. Customer queries soared, even though B&W had mailed everyone with information about the changeover. Then, following the transfer of ownership, staff had to handle the enormous task of transferring various funds and making payouts to account holders.

During the run-up to the sale completion, B&W had to employ over 400 temporary staff as well as assign large numbers of employees to various change projects. B&W estimates that it used 30–40% more resources than anticipated.

Companies may not have access to the spring of eternal youth to help rid themselves of their Achilles heel, but an effective communication process can be a powerful restorative when it:

◪ reinforces the strategic vision and objectives of the M&A;
◪ helps employees feel involved in what is happening;
◪ helps employees feel that their views count;
◪ percolates fresh ideas and insights throughout the organisation.

In many M&As the opposite is often true during the run-up period. Senior managers, for example, may become remote and uncommunicative, perhaps because they are exhausted by the M&A or perhaps because they do not have any answers to give employees who are worried about their future.

According to consultancy Watson Wyatt's worldwide M&A study 1998/99 (see below), poor communication has a direct impact on employees' commitment and willingness to co-operate. Non-communication, under-communication or thoughtless communication is translated in people's minds along the following lines: "they never speak to us" becomes "they don't care about us", which must mean "they don't understand us" or "they think we're stupid", so it must be true that "they're going to get rid of us", and if that's the case "I think they are stupid" and "I don't trust them", which leads ultimately to "I'm not going to co-operate".

Further work by AMR, a London-based research consultancy, yields a similarly bleak picture. In a survey of merged companies, 74% of respondents believed that their communication plans were insufficiently considered. AMR cites Fuchs, a German oil company, as a spectacular example of a failure to communicate. It was not until six months after its acquisition of Century Oils that Fuchs began to communicate how it planned to run the company. "Morale collapsed, employees left and performance had still not met expectations five years after the acquisition."

But in M&As the flow of communication is usually from the top/centre of the organisation through to the "rank and file". There is often little upward feedback except for, say, surveys that seek to unearth information about employee motivation and retention.

Communication woes of M&As

Watson Wyatt's 1998/99 M&A survey reveals that although respondents listed effective communications as the second most important contributor to a successful M&A integration, only 4% said that it was given top priority during integration. Only 43% said their communication efforts were successful. The main reasons for ineffective communications were:

- inadequate resources
- too slow
- inadequate senior management attention

- not all groups were communicated with
- inconsistent messages
- launched too late
- not well planned
- not frequent enough
- ended too early.

Guiding principles

Communications processes should be built on the following principles.

Build on the best of both worlds

Assess the quality or cultural suitability of the communications processes of both businesses, and build on best practice wherever it is found. Do not adopt a "conquering heroes" approach and automatically implement your preferred mode of communication.

Assess existing communication processes not just in the light of operational efficiency, cost and flexibility, but also to determine what important cultural values and attitudes they reflect. This is critical in cross-cultural mergers where there may be huge differences in styles of communication (for example, some cultures value "plain speaking" and others favour a more diffuse and indirect style). In simple terms, communication processes give revealing clues about an organisation's preference for:

- formality versus informality;
- written communication versus face-to-face;
- instruction versus debate and feedback;
- centralised versus devolved.

An M&A communication process that disregards one company's preferred style of communication will be widely seen to be directly assaulting its values and culture. Only a small amount of sensitivity and flexibility is needed to avoid this pitfall. For example, in companies that value discussion, meetings can be planned after every formal merger communication to give people an opportunity to have their say.

Tightly link communications to the strategy and integration process

Communications are an inherent part of the integration process – not a stand-alone process that is somehow peripheral to the real job of integration. A communication process must be tightly linked to the merger strategy. It must consistently and frequently reaffirm the short-term and long-term goals of the new business. For example, if the combined companies want to create a more global business, communications should reflect this by accommodating different communication styles; giving coverage to integration activities in different geographical regions; including senior managers from all the regions, not just head office; and creating linkages through networking opportunities and other forums to enable different parts of the business to share their expertise and insights.

Assign a senior manager to both oversee and champion the communications process. This helps ensure that senior managers have sufficient involvement in getting the message across and can adapt it should any changes occur that require a shift in business strategy or a change in the integration plan. Having a senior person champion communications also sends important messages about the company's desire to inform and involve all employees.

Make sure that the communication process is aligned with the new model of the organisation. For example, when the new business is likely to be devolved and integration is being managed primarily at a divisional level rather than from the centre, coherent decisions must be made on who is responsible for what in the communications process. What is the role of the centre: is it responsible for controlling information? Is it there to pass on information to the devolved communications teams? Or is its prime function to gather information about integration activities in order to present a view of the whole company?

Make sure that communication is aligned with the desired degree of integration and collaboration. For example, if the combined businesses tie their operations together, communication processes should aim to help employees understand the components of the combined business, highlight working practices and processes that will be changed or adopted and target teams and divisions that are most likely to start working together. If cultural integration is desired, communication processes should concentrate on highlighting the values of the combined business, using appropriate individuals to get important cultural messages across and act as role models of desired behaviours, and to help employees explore cultural differences and new ways of working.

Do it every which way
Communication should not simply flow from the top/centre of the new

business. Although employees need to know about how the M&A is progressing, downward communication is simply "telling" employees and does little on its own to win trust and commitment or to ensure that the knowledge within the two organisations is being fed back into the emergent strategy. In M&As, trust and collaboration is built through continuous dialogue. Communication processes need to flow in all directions: up and down, and side to side. Employees should have opportunities to say how well integration is proceeding and what barriers or problems need to be resolved. These insights act as valuable "reality checks" for managers who have become out of touch with what is going on at the business coalface. Upward feedback also helps to show employees that their views count. Side-to-side communication is important between people that need to pool their expertise at certain times but that may not necessarily work together closely.

The communication process should be based on the different levels of employee engagement described below.

Rules of engagement

Co-ordination

The first level of any M&A communication programme is to inform employees (and stakeholders such as suppliers, customers and strategic partners) about what is likely to happen and what the immediate impact is likely to be. Before they even begin to think about whether and how they might contribute to the new business, employees must be informed as quickly as possible about a number of factors, ranging from individual concerns to business-wide issues.

- Changes in terms and conditions.
- Whether they are likely to lose their job or be relocated.
- The personal M&A timetable, detailing when or if the M&A is likely to affect the individual's role, function, job scope, working processes or reporting lines.
- The general integration timetable. Focus groups with employees reveal that even when employees are not directly affected by the M&A, they still need to be kept informed about what is happening throughout the business. Without this information, they often feel cut off and forgotten.
- The "big picture". People need to be constantly reminded of the desired end state of the integration process.

Communication methods to be considered for the above include:

- detailed instructions and documentation;
- face-to-face meetings with line managers and human-resources specialists;
- corporate magazines and other forms of merger updates, such as bulletins, telephone helplines and e-mail question-and-answer forums;
- regular updates from senior managers, which help employees feel they are getting merger news "hot off the press".

Co-operation

Communication processes should focus on impediments that cause people to opt out of the integration process. They must create opportunities for employees to voice their questions and concerns. This stage of engagement is primarily about getting intellectual buy-in. Communication processes should:

- repeatedly state the rationale for the combination – employees who are going through stressful changes may not be able to grasp the business case until their personal working life is more settled;
- emphasise the compelling reasons for change and why a combination was preferred to other strategic options such as strategic alliances or joint ventures;
- discourage employees from trying to convince themselves that "things will return to normal" by reinforcing senior managers' commitment to the new venture and to developing new ways of working;
- reaffirm positive messages about the benefits of the combination (while still acknowledging unpleasant events such as site closures, enforced divestments and redundancies). As Bristol & West's Mr Flanagan comments:
  Even in our situation, when no job losses were involved, people couldn't quite believe our assurances, making it necessary to keep repeating the message.
- translate lofty statements about merger synergies into more concrete and understandable terms;
- break down merger goals into specific milestones and objectives for different parts of the business and group these into specific

timeframes, ranging from the first few weeks of the combination to the first three, then six months;

◪ combat internal "navel gazing" or a refusal to accept the need for change by supplying information about the external business environment and competitive threats and opportunities.

Appropriate communication methods include:

◪ anonymous billboards, where employees can write their views and comments;
◪ telephone and e-mail helplines;
◪ regular newsletters and bulletins;
◪ circulation of press articles and stockmarket information;
◪ round-table discussions;
◪ road shows and various presentations by senior managers, including question-and-answer sessions;
◪ divisional briefings and departmental or team meetings to discuss the implications of the combination;
◪ training and development events focusing on required new skills.

Collaboration

Communication processes at this level should aim to get people's emotional engagement while reinforcing their intellectual buy-in. Collaboration also entails breaking down barriers between the combining organisations so that people can begin to explore their differences and similarities, appreciate complementary skills and experience (which requires acknowledging weaknesses or gaps in expertise) and begin to see the merits of collaboration. Communication processes can help nurture collaborative working by:

◪ highlighting examples of successful collaboration, especially when this helps achieve a specific goal of the combination or it leads to successful innovation;
◪ ensuring senior managers and leaders continue to articulate their vision for the combining business and spell out in concrete terms the importance of collaborative working;
◪ providing a platform for influential "change agents" who are willing to champion collaborative values;
◪ encouraging mutual respect and learning by disseminating the

insights and experiences of different teams throughout the organisation.

Communication methods to be considered for the above include:

- bulletins and newsletters;
- internal seminars;
- networking events bringing together different parts of the business;
- senior management presentations;
- internal reward schemes for innovation and collaborative working.

Commitment

When sufficient commitment to collaboration has been achieved and widespread levels of trust exist between the people in the combining organisations, the communications process should shift its focus to concentrate on "normal" business and operational issues.

Celebrations

The day a firm merges or is acquired is a critical one. It is like a rite of passage as employees realise that their company has changed forever and that a new era is beginning. Surprisingly, when the day comes, it can be an anticlimax. Hence the importance of celebrating this rite of passage.

M&A celebrations can be grand affairs. When Price Waterhouse and Coopers & Lybrand became PricewaterhouseCoopers, a generous budget was given to its offices around the world to celebrate what was termed "Programme Day One". Although the central merger team ensured that the new name was launched simultaneously around the world (marketing materials were prepared by the centre and translated into nine languages), different nationalities chose to celebrate the changeover in different ways. For example, some 6,000 employees in the United States shared breakfast in New York's Central Park, employees in the Netherlands held beach parties and employees in Germany held an evening fireworks display. Ed Smith, the partner responsible for providing steerage from the centre, comments:

Our approach was to enable celebrations to be as local as possible, yet also to recognise that the global leadership had some messages about the future of the new organisation and its name and brand. The celebrations were very successful and proved a big emotional anchor in the first week of the merger.

Humbler celebrations are no less important. Employees of an acquired American company, for instance, erected a "memory board", where they put pictures of various events and people that helped shape the history and identity of the business. When Leeds Building Society was acquired by Halifax, employees gathered to watch the company name being taken down from the front of the building and then went inside to collect various artefacts such as pens, business cards and identity cards that carried the company name and logo.

Holding some sort of celebration is often a cathartic experience for everyone concerned. People have the opportunity both to mourn their former organisations and to celebrate its history and achievements. Rituals such as removing logos and other "cultural icons" can be a helpful way of making the changeover a reality to still shell-shocked employees. The outpouring of emotion and the camaraderie among employees can also help people to brace themselves for whatever uncertainties the future holds.

7 Minimising the fallout: the immediate transition

BUSINESS TRANSITIONS are notoriously difficult to manage success-fully, and M&As represent one of the most difficult because of the level and pace of change involved. Work by Duncan Angwin, a merger specialist at Warwick Business School in the UK,[1] reveals that:

- 40% of all change takes place in the first two months of an M&A;
- more than half of this change, ie more than 20%, immediately follows completion;
- change continues at a high but rapidly declining level for the remainder of the first six months;
- at the end of nine months, more than 80% of all changes will have been initiated.

The M&A process is highly stressful and leads to anxiety, cynicism, anger and depression among those involved in it. Well-laid plans can easily be swept away in the maelstrom of emotions and impulses that cause employees to act in unpredictable and irrational ways. Many employees become preoccupied about seemingly trivial details, such as whether they will still have a space in the company car park. They also become unaccountably fond of their former organisation, its habits, eccentricities and former management, even when they regularly criti-cised these things before the M&A.

Managing the immediate human fallout of the transition is as impor-tant as developing an effective integration process and plan. Chapter 5 discussed integration using the metaphor of a nucleus. Integration teams, it was argued, must function as the "positively charged" centre of the emerging organisation. This chapter highlights how the strain of the immediate transition can "irradiate" the creative potential of the com-bining businesses and goes on to outline how to avoid that happening.

Free-fall dangers

The human fallout of a merger or acquisition can be shocking, and many integration teams are unprepared for it. Just because the manage-ment teams of the combining organisations support the changeover, it does not mean that the rest of the workforce will fall into line.

Many studies demonstrate that any merger or acquisition will unleash "psychological shock waves" that will ripple through the combining organisations and trigger a series of unforeseen consequences. Mitchell Lee Marks and Philip Mirvis,[2] two M&A experts, argue that a merger or acquisition, no matter how amicable, is a seismic event, resulting in a climate of ambiguity in which trust levels decline and people put more emphasis on self-preservation. This "merger syndrome" gives rise to six common problems:

- deteriorating communication;
- poor productivity;
- increased parochialism and less team play;
- power struggles;
- reduced commitment to corporate goals;
- a tendency to bail out by leaving the organisation.

Unless integration teams and operational managers take steps to combat the immediate shock and uncertainty triggered by changeover, the combining businesses can become caught in a vicious cycle, as seen in Chart 7.1 on the next page.

Various studies suggest that mergers do not lead to growth in revenue but quite the opposite. Cox School of Business at Southern Methodist University in America, in a study of 193 mergers completed between 1990 and 1997, found that only 37% of the acquired companies maintained the same rate of revenue growth in the first quarter after the merger announcement. After nine months, only 11% had the same or a better rate of revenue growth than before the merger. The study concluded that unsettled customers and distracted staff were the reason for this drop in performance.

The performance of the new business is affected by four reactions following the merger.

- **Widespread anxiety.** Employees are distracted and spend much time discussing the change, speculating about potential redundancies and constructing worst-case scenarios. Almost every employee, regardless of their role, seniority or ability, fears for their job security, and many start polishing their CVs.
- **Organisational paralysis.** Normal planning cycles are disrupted as managers become uncertain about basic parameters they are

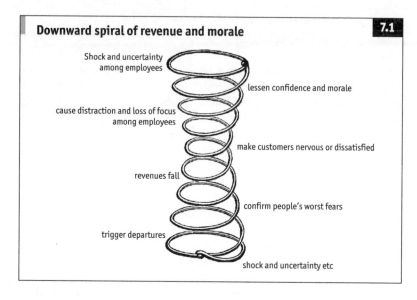

Downward spiral of revenue and morale   **7.1**

Shock and uncertainty among employees

lessen confidence and morale

cause distraction and loss of focus among employees

make customers nervous or dissatisfied

revenues fall

confirm people's worst fears

trigger departures

shock and uncertainty etc

working to such as budgets and performance targets. Investment plans are put on hold until the management structure is fully in place. Strategic alliances are blighted by the possibility that they may be reviewed or even dispensed with.

◪ **Loss of leadership.** Until they feel secure about their position in the combined business, managers are often wary of doing anything that carries a risk of failure for fear that this will blight their career prospects. Similarly, they are unwilling to push forward new business developments for fear that their decisions will be reversed or that they will lose the authority and resources necessary to deliver their promises.

◪ **Rising levels of customer dissatisfaction.** Organisational drift does not take long to have an impact on customer service. The employees who deal with customers are more uncertain and less confident about what they can promise to customers. They may also communicate their anxieties or negative feelings about the new set up.

Matthias Bekier, Anna Bogardus and Tim Oldham, McKinsey consultants in Australia, have spelt out what the financial consequences can be.[3] Using the Cox study and their own research into 160 acquisitions between 1995 and 1996, they have calculated that if the newly combined business's revenue growth is only 1% lower than projected, it would require cuts in costs that are 25% higher than it had originally planned to make up the shortfall. Conversely, if target revenue growth is exceeded by 2–3%, that can offset cost cuts that are 50% lower than predicted.

Revenue matters greatly to combining businesses. As the McKinsey consultants explain:

> *Ultimately, it is revenue that determines the outcome of the merger, not costs; whatever the merger's objectives, revenue actually hits the bottom line harder. Fluctuations in revenue can quickly outweigh fluctuations in planned cost savings ... The temptation is then to make excessively deep cuts or cuts in inappropriate places, thus depressing future earnings by taking out muscle, not just fat.*

(See McKinsey's suggestions on how to protect revenue below.)

Value-generating activities

A priority must be to protect revenue and devote as much managerial expertise as possible in the first three months to achieving revenue growth. The McKinsey consultants offer the following advice.

- Treat revenue growth as rigorously as cost cutting.
- "Hard wire" cost disciplines at every level of the integration process to help senior managers focus on revenue.
- Look after existing customers and revenue – target and retain "revenue-generating talent", especially those who handle relations with customers.
- Instil a performance culture geared for growth by using every means, especially "entrepreneurial, well-mentored teams with ambitious targets and incentives".

Disappearing talent

Much of the energy of a newly combined business can be sapped by a steady exodus of valued employees in the first two or three months of its existence. A survey of 12 "serial" acquirers by Best Practices, an American consultancy, found that more than one-third of managers and talented technical employees typically leave after a company is acquired.

In investment banking, Donaldson, Lufkin & Jenrette (DLJ) lost most of its most valued employees after being acquired by Credit Suisse in September 2000. Within a few months, Ken Moelis, who had played an important role in making DLJ a leading junk-bond underwriter, went off to join rival USB, taking six of his colleagues with him. Another senior manager from DLJ became the new co-head of mergers at Bear Stearns, and a number of DLJ employees were recruited by Deutsche-Alex Brown.

The merger between JP Morgan and Chase Manhattan saw a similar exodus, with Goldman Sachs being one of the biggest beneficiaries during the first year of the merged bank. *The Economist*[4] estimated that the biggest winner in the investment banking M&A fallout had been Lehman Brothers. It reported that during 2000, the firm increased its workforce by 25% to over 11,000 by cherry picking staff from Salomon Brothers after its absorption into Citigroup as well as from JP Morgan and Chase. Lehman Brothers also hired 250 people from DLJ.

Control factors

Often departures of valued employees are the result of political fighting over who has real control of the combination. For example, when Morgan Stanley, headed by John Mack, merged in 1997 with Dean Whitter, headed by Philip Purcell, it was widely understood that Mr Mack had agreed to become president of the merged bank only on the proviso that he would succeed Mr Purcell as chief executive. However, according to *The Economist*,[5] when Mr Mack said in March 2001 that the time had come for him to become CEO, Mr Purcell refused to step down and successfully persuaded the board to support him. Mr Mack immediately resigned.

In any M&A there is always a risk (or certainty) that talented individuals will defect to the enemy camp, bringing valuable knowledge about their former organisation. When AOL and Time Warner merged, Richard Bressler, Time Warner's chief financial officer, who had been highly instrumental in pushing for the merger but was unhappy with the operational job that he was given in the new organisation, quickly departed to become the new CFO at rival media company Viacom.

The damage such departures do

As well as potentially damaging the business's competitive position, departures of talented and highly regarded individuals can have the following effects:

■ Damage the business's capacity to create a culture that encourages experimentation and fresh thinking. If departing individuals are widely perceived as innovative and highly capable people, their departure may be interpreted as a signal that the emerging culture does not easily tolerate "disruptive" people who are willing to push the boundaries of thinking.

■ Lead to the loss of a valuable group, which can become the loss of a core capability. For example, the day after Mr Mack departed from Morgan Stanley, the head of the bank's international private clients group left to join Bank of America. This triggered widespread concerns about Morgan Stanley's future performance. According to *The Economist*:[6]

> One of the many concerns raised ... was that Mr Purcell's background as a consultant for McKinsey might lay bare a weakness in investment banking, where Mr Mack had responsibility.

■ Cause an imbalance in that, if high-level departures are from only one of the combining organisations, employees of that organisation are likely to feel threatened. Their resulting lack of engagement with – or even antagonism to – the combined business will therefore in turn threaten that organisation. As they see their former leaders leave, remaining employees feel that their influence and stake in the new business has diminished. They become less willing and able to contribute, intellectually or emotionally. It becomes a much harder task to gain their commitment and trust. Such was the discovery of Glaxo Wellcome, as Elaine Davis, director of human-resources services, recounts:

> Significant numbers of the senior management and leadership of the acquired company left, and employees ... that were still with us and going through the selection process felt that they didn't have access to the chain of command at Glaxo. I think, in a sense, they felt powerless to be heard. Despite our best communication efforts, I think that they were suspicious and cynical.[7]

■ Undermine cultural capabilities. In past deals, many senior managers, particularly those of the acquired business, were swiftly removed because it was assumed that this would speed up cultural integration. It is now thought that a cultural vacuum or confusion is more likely to be created, with damaging consequences. Combining organisations are much more likely to recognise that each partner's culture constitutes part of its value and unique capability. Corporate culture contains collective experiences, insights, learning, mindsets, values and know-how that help transform individual skills into collective capability. When a cadre of managers and leaders suddenly leave, this "cultural capability" can be diluted, distorted or lost.

Remaining employees who feel culturally threatened are likely to try to protect their culture from further damage and resist any form of cultural change. Work by Rikard Larsson[8] reveals that this resistance can be both active and passive.

- Separate "maintenance mechanisms": employees maintain their own cultures by "intensified conversation" where they glorify their past and vilify their new partner. This becomes a collective defence mechanism and helps exaggerate the magnitude of the threat to the group's culture.
- "Collective learned helplessness": when one of the combining organisations perceives itself as the "weaker" partner, it experiences a collective loss of self-esteem. This causes a sense of helplessness and depression. This shared response can eventually become "demoralising and disabling". The capacity for collective learning is seriously undermined, as is the ability to adjust to the new environment.

Engineering the positive

For any business transformation to occur, a critical mass of employees must be involved, not just a small echelon of highly capable individuals or senior managers. Ordinary people are capable of extraordinary things when they are energised and motivated to make a difference in their immediate work environment. But to accept the challenge, most people need to be convinced that their leaders genuinely value them and that their insights and ideas will be heard and respected. Finding ways to switch on employees and to energise and motivate them is the essence of managing a newly merged business. Here is how it can be done.

Co-ordination: helping people understand where they fit

There needs to be a co-ordinated policy that tackles people's worries about their future and answers such questions as:

- Do I still have a job?
- How will my pay and benefits be affected?
- Will I be relocated?
- Will I be assigned a new role and position, or must I apply for internal posts?
- Who will be my new boss?

In complex M&AS, it may not be possible to answer some or all of these questions for several months, in which case it is best to be open about the lack of hard information. As soon as possible, each individual should be given a personal timetable, detailing when decisions will be made about their position, role, terms and conditions. "Transparency" is important in explaining how staffing decisions will be made in the new business. For an example of four different processes and their relative merits, see "Employee selection" on the next page.

Employees who are left in limbo for months, not knowing whether their jobs will continue or be redesigned, either leave the company or join the ranks of the "walking wounded". For example, in a merger between two leading British retailers, some branches had to wait as long as two years before knowing for sure whether they would stay open and be "rebadged". Interviews with the staff of one London store revealed great bitterness at the way they had to rely on "signs and wonders" in order to guess their fate. The warehouse manager comments:

> We all felt excited and positive at the time of the
> announcement, but then everything went quiet. Things just
> plodded along. We didn't see much of our new managers and
> they gave us little feedback about what was going on.

About three months after the announcement, senior managers met store managers and told them that some 23 branches would need to be closed. The branch manager says:

> The gap in communication was too long. To make it worse,
> none of us knew for months whether our store would close. It
> was only after "rebadging" that my branch knew we would
> stay open.

According to the store manager, staff had divined that there were three levels of rebadging. He explains:

There was a full rebadging, when the store was completely refurbished – then you knew you were safe. There was partial rebadging, where the new logo was put up and the point-of-sale cardboard name was replaced – then you hoped you still had a job but you couldn't be quite sure. Then there was what we called "lip-service" conversion, where the minimum was done, perhaps the store was given the new logo and new uniforms only – then people got really worried.

The branch's customer services supervisor sums up the feeling of the branch staff when she comments:

I don't think our new management team have a clue about what we have gone through and all the changes we have gone through under our former owners and now this. They never seem to listen. They think they know best. Why don't they come in and ask us what we think? They could learn so much.

Plainly, the absence of specific information from the new owners became a major impediment to the employees at the store, who became demoralised and alienated. That they still wanted to contribute to the new business is a testament to the tenacity of human beings. Ironically, it was the best-performing store in the former business and their jobs were never under threat.

Employee selection: getting the "best of both"

Business combinations that seek to transform their operations into a stronger, more capable organisation have four selection options, according to Ira Kay, managing director of the global compensation practice at consultancy Watson Wyatt, and Mike Shelton of McKinsey.

1 *New leader.* A single leader is appointed for each line and functional area. He or she selects the unit's team from the existing combined workforce. The advantage of this process is that it is usually speedy and efficient since it is in the leader's best interest to pick the most capable people. However, the manager may not have sufficient knowledge of the other company's people, inviting the danger of "cronyism". He or she should have the opportunity to develop first-hand knowledge of the other company's candidates and perhaps receive the help of

independent management appraisers.

2 *Two in the box.* Both companies provide an individual for each business area and the two work together to construct a team. The advantage is that they can pool their knowledge of suitable candidates. The disadvantage is that there may be tensions between the two leaders, especially when it becomes clear who will ultimately be the new leader.

3 *Independent management appraisal.* A neutral third party, perhaps a recruitment agency, appraises candidates and then makes recommendations. The advantage is that the judgment should be objective, help minimise fears of favouritism and be useful in situations where there is no obvious candidate. However, the process can be time-consuming and employees may resent "outsiders" and believe that their bosses are in a better position to assess them.

4 *Post and invite.* All available posts are advertised internally. The advantage is that capable people can be discovered. The disadvantage is that it is time-consuming, and it also sends the message that people may lose their jobs, encouraging more talented people to go job hunting.

Typically, best-of-both approaches are used to select people for the first three echelons and take 18–24 weeks. Staffing the rest of the organisation usually takes an additional 8–16 weeks.

Source: Kay, I. and Shelton, M., "The people problem in mergers",
McKinsey Quarterly, No. 4, 2000.

Some companies attach the greatest importance to informing their staff, even in complex, lengthy integration programmes. BP Amoco, for example, undertook to inform employees within 30 days of finalising the merger whether they would keep their jobs, keep them only for the short term, or be made redundant immediately.

Senior management appointments need to be made speedily to minimise political infighting and to ensure that leaders are in place who are ready and able to focus everyone's attention on the core business.

Early announcements of redundancies are the most effective means of reducing anxiety. They also help to ensure that everyone's attention is soon focused on growth opportunities, rather than on cost-cutting measures. Equally important is to ensure that "outgoing" employees are treated well. Using outplacement services can be a good way of ensuring that redundant staff find new jobs quickly, and this also sends the important message to remaining employees that the merged business

Chart 7.2 **Cost savings delivered by M&As**

Sector	% of companies surveyed
Head-count reduction	66
Buying and merchandising	60
Supply chain	60
Procurement	48
Manufacturing	35
Warehousing/distribution	32
New product development	32
Outsourcing	25
Research and development	24

Source: KPMG, *Unlocking shareholder value: the keys to success*, 1999.

values all its employees. Glaxo Wellcome discovered to its cost that keeping employees in limbo is the worst option. Employees were required to apply for their positions and, if they failed to be reselected, were placed in a selection pool so that they could be considered for other internal jobs. Steve Sons, director of organisational effectiveness, recalls:

> That turned out to be a nightmare. It was referred to as "the drowning pool". If you got in the pool it was a horrible thing and most people would rather have been let go.[9]

Job losses and strategic considerations

In mergers that have been driven by consolidation or economies of scale, redundancies are an inevitable consequence. Work by consultancy KPMG[10] reveals that head-count reduction is the most common means by which companies achieve cost reductions during a merger or acquisition (see Chart 7.2).

Redundancies are the main way that merged companies make cost savings. However, when the success of a merger depends on engaging employees, managers often grapple with the following dilemmas.

◪ If growth is the main objective, will an immediate round of redundancies seriously undermine and distort this message? The task of building trust could be made much harder. Those managing the integration process are more likely to be viewed as "slash-and-burn" teams with a hidden agenda to close down sections and even whole departments. Employees may be much less likely to co-operate, and even less willing to collaborate by sharing knowledge and expertise. Messages about business growth could generate waves of cynicism against the backdrop of redundancies.

◪ Will talented employees inadvertently be let go? Although due diligence should have identified a number of talented employees, this list is unlikely to be exhaustive and highly likely to be biased towards managerial staff. Other important players will become apparent as the combining organisations work to understand more subtle aspects of each other's strengths and capabilities. For example, in an acquired British merchant bank, consultants who were called in to help re-engineer the bank's spaghetti-like back-office processes discovered to their horror that there was only one employee who understood how all the processes fitted together, and he was a reclusive and eccentric individual who might normally have been included in a redundancy programme. In the event, he played a pivotal role in helping the investment bank streamline its operations.

◪ Will relationships with customers be disrupted? Business success increasingly relies on retaining customers and building relationships with them. Could staff redundancies undermine these relationships or cause customers to have a negative perception of the new business? Could vital "relational" information be lost? First Union, an American bank, burned its fingers when it acquired Corestate, a bank in Pennsylvania. It slashed Corestate's staff to such a degree that services were affected and customers defected. When First Union announced its intention to acquire Wachovia Bank in April 2001, it made clear its intention to proceed carefully with job losses. The bank promised no job losses for one year and then said that it would lay off 8% of the total number of jobs gradually over time.

◪ Will alliance relationships be disrupted? Research into strategic alliances[11] reveals that the success of many different forms of strategic alliances relies far more on a delicate tissue of relationships between individuals in the partnering organisations than on the formal controls, systems and processes that outwardly define the alliance. Alliances work well when an inner core of individuals find ways of building trust and co-operation. These people have the ability to network and create a shared culture and working style. They may not fill managerial posts or appear important in any alliance management chart, yet their input is crucial. Companies that get rid of these people place their alliances in peril.

When Halifax acquired the Leeds Building Society, it opted for a policy of no job losses. Ignoring pressure from the financial community to achieve instant cost savings through head-count reductions, Halifax's management team were united in their belief that job losses would cause divisiveness, distract the new business from achieving ambitious growth plans and reduce the success of future acquisitions. The result was overmanning for a period of time, especially in the bank's head office, but Halifax's managers believed this was a price worth paying as employees remained reasonably positive and open to change during the merger, a view confirmed by focus groups with employees conducted by the author. Although some employees opted for voluntary redundancy, the majority of "displaced" employees were, as Alan McAvan, then employee development manager, comments, "reasonably willing to be in limbo for a time. We assured them that we wouldn't disown them but would do our best to match their skills with vacant jobs as they arose". These employees were given assurances that their terms and conditions would remain protected for five years, even if they were eventually placed in a lower-graded position.

The big issue of pay and benefits

Changes in pay and benefits are another important consideration for employees and have the potential to cause great disruption. Chapter 4 outlined how employers are obliged to inform and consult with employees when they are being transferred to the acquiring organisation on their existing terms and conditions. If an acquisition does not involve a transfer of undertakings, employers are normally required to consult with their employees about any changes to their terms and conditions, and if trade unions are involved, this can become a lengthy process. To minimise the possibilities of internal wrangles, it is advisable to allocate plenty of resources to the task, including the temporary use of independent compensation advisers.

Changes in benefits – which these days include life insurance, pensions, medical cover, stock or stock options, paid time off, flexible hours, luncheon vouchers, help with nursery care, school fees or elderly care – can whip up much emotion among employees. Human-resources managers at PricewaterhouseCoopers found that the two accountancy firms had a large number of benefits, and any attempt to slim down the options caused great resentment. In the end, the solution was to create a flexible "menu" system where employees could please themselves.

In straightforward mergers, human-resources managers and line managers should be available to talk through the details of any new arrangements as early as possible. Where a new compensation and benefits structure is to be introduced, or employees are being transferred to the other company's scheme, employees should be told when they will receive detailed information. Then they should receive some form of compensation chart that shows them in an understandable way how their pay and benefits have been adjusted, including details of transitional arrangements. There should be openness about why decisions affecting individual employees or groups of employees have been made.

Those with experience of successful M&As will testify to the importance of being willing to listen to the concerns of employees and negotiate with them over the provision of specific benefits. Companies like Internet network provider Cisco Systems have sometimes learnt the hard way. Cisco acquired Stratacom in 1996. Within a few months, almost one-third of Stratacom's sales force quit because they lost accounts to Cisco people and because of changes to their commission plan. In its more recent acquisition of Cerent, Cisco took the decision to allow Cerent's salesforce to keep their accounts, even if they overlapped with those of their new owner. In other acquisitions, Cisco increased salaries and expense accounts to keep employees of the acquired business motivated and focused.

"Nuts and bolts" work issues, such as business cards, car-park places, the provision of cafeteria and luncheon vouchers and other perks and benefits, are often viewed as unimportant details, yet they have the potential to cause enormous resentment and dissatisfaction. In the case of acquisitions that will remain operationally separate, experienced acquirers recommend moving quickly to "rebadge" the business. These types of acquisitions are amenable to "quick-hit" approaches, with the highest priority being to reassure staff about their terms and conditions and future career prospects (see "Cisco and Cerent" on the next page).

Cisco and Cerent: a rapid transfer

At Cisco, a full-time centralised integration team works hard between announcement and completion to ensure a rapid transfer of employment. The company follows a simple formula. Typically, product-engineering and marketing groups remain as independent business units, and sales and manufacturing units are absorbed into existing Cisco departments.

The day after announcing its acquisition of Cerent, for example, Cisco's 23-member central integration team met Cerent managers to begin planning the changeover. The combined team systematically mapped all Cerent's 400 employees into a Cisco post. The majority of Cerent people stayed in the same posts, but around 30 employees were reassigned because of overlaps with Cisco. On the first day of the new combination, the integration team issued every employee with a job title, boss, bonus plan, health plan and direct link to Cisco's internal website. Later in the day they were issued with new identity cards, and by mid-week they all had new business cards.

The only hitch in this streamlined process was the mugs with "welcome to Cisco" that were discovered by staff working in the distribution function before Cisco met Cerent staff to announce the M&A.

Co-operation

Efforts to encourage co-operation can be overshadowed by the continual need to deal with issues that are concerned with co-ordination, such as pay and benefits, redundancies, appointments and job transfers. These issues absorb huge swathes of time. They typically require the attention of senior managers and integration teams. They have the potential to disrupt the business, trigger employee disputes and cause unwanted departures. But resolving them does not automatically motivate staff or gain their support. Other routes must be taken to promote co-operation. In complex mergers, leaders should intermittently review whether they are spending too much time on the mechanics of the changeover and not enough on building support for the new business.

Once employees understand their roles and positions in the combined business, they can begin to focus on the business itself and the various challenges involved in the changeover. This stage requires managers to move from "tell" mode to "sell" mode – to persuade everyone of the merits of the combination and its long-term potential. Senior managers, and especially the executive directors, should hold regular meetings with employees to get across:

◪ the strategic objectives of the combination;
◪ the need for change;
◪ the envisaged synergies;
◪ the immediate performance goals for the combined business.

Gaining people's co-operation does not require sophisticated techniques or the application of rocket science. What it does require is good, old-fashioned leadership – a willingness to meet people in a variety of forums, to argue the business case, answer questions, vigorously debate issues and constantly emphasise the potential benefits of the combination – in both business and personal terms.

Xerox managers work intensively to communicate the business case for the company's acquisitions. In the first few weeks, the company typically uses a variety of methods to explain to employees the logic of the M&A and to solicit their views. Global operational and human-resources managers hold round-table discussions. Division presidents provide regular updates about the combination through a weekly telephone recording. A question-and-answer website is also available. Integration teams around the world hold weekly conference calls to discuss any issue that employees view as important.

Xerox and other companies know that employees have an insatiable appetite for information about how the integration programme is proceeding. A steady drip of information about changes helps to maintain momentum and to impose logic and coherence to the sometimes hectic pace of change. Employees are also more likely to be won over when they see the merger progressing to plan. Celebrating success and even small achievements are important means of creating a positive climate.

Encouraging co-operation among employees is a delicate task and represents the first small step towards creating trust between the combining organisations. Broken promises at this stage only encourage cynicism and suspicion.

Allianz, a German insurer, just one week after it completed its purchase in 2001 of Dresdner Bank, reneged on a commitment to grant Dresdner's investment bank, Dresdner Kleinwort Wasserstein, its own stockmarket listing. Allianz argued that the turmoil of equity markets meant that DrKW would not be able to build up a strong enough track record over the next year or two to make it an attractive candidate for an independent stockmarket quote. However, financial analysts had already questioned the feasibility of achieving such a technically and legally complicated step of slicing away Dresdner's corporate lending business. Whether or not employees accepted the justifications of their new owners, it is unlikely that the change of course helped build trust or co-operation.

Some firms have turned to remuneration as a means of "buying" staff loyalty during the immediate transition. Oracle offers options to the staff of small high-technology firms it has acquired. Furthermore, a group bonus is awarded over a six-month period if the acquisition meets its new performance targets. Loyalty bonuses are also offered to certain individuals if they remain with Oracle for a period usually lasting six months to one year after the acquisition.

The wave of consolidations among investment banks has led to substantial increases in remuneration that may prove to be unsustainable. For example, *The Economist* reported in 2000[12] that leading investment banks were resorting to huge bonuses to both recruit and retain talented people. Credit Suisse First Boston (CSFB) reportedly retained one telecoms analyst by offering her a three-year package worth more than $5m a year. Both Goldman Sachs and Donaldson, Lufkin & Jenrette gave junior staff a 25% pay rise. Deutsche Bank recruited an asset-backed securities team from CSFB by doubling their pay.

Financial incentives are not a solution in companies where highly valued employees are tied in with stocks and shares and stand to become paper millionaires. Cisco, for that reason, refuses to acquire companies where employees have "golden parachutes", sometimes known as accelerated vesting, that award them substantial payouts should their company be acquired. Charles Giancarlo, who worked for a time on Cisco's M&A activities, says:

> The minute you buy the company, they all get rich. We prefer "golden handcuffs". These are applied with two-year non-compete agreements with key executives and technical staff of the acquired company, as well as Cisco stock options that vest over time.

But financial incentives can be used for only a small minority, or the business will saddle itself with crippling costs. Watson Wyatt's Mr Kay comments: "Generally, retention incentives add 5–10% to the total cost of the deal – enough to wreck it."

It is also worth bearing in mind that financial incentives are a necessary but not sufficient source of motivation. Watson Wyatt's annual survey on how employers retain talented people makes this clear. Only 25% of employers thought that rewards motivated people enough to make a discernible impact on the performance of the business.[13]

Attracting and retaining talent

A smaller survey by Stanton Marris, a British consultancy, sheds further light on the importance of financial incentives to talented employees.[14] Based on 150 interviews with talented people and company representatives, the report concludes:

> *Money is important, but not a primary motivator ... The needs of talented people are transactional (good pay, benefits, etc) as well as emotional (feeling valued, trusted, challenged, recognised, etc) ... Competitive advantage increasingly needs to come from managing the emotional side of the employment relationship.*

The report produces an enlightening list of priorities that help engage talented people.

- **Professional challenge and growth.** Talented people want to learn and be challenged. They want to grow through being placed in challenging roles where they need to develop new skills. They welcome organisational support through mentoring, coaching, development and training.
- **Career progression.** Talented individuals, especially younger ones, take responsibility for their own career paths, but look for signs that their company is committed to their career development.
- **Freedom.** The level of freedom desired by talented people varies slightly according to their career stages, but they generally want their organisations to trust them and be willing to "take a risk" by giving them "head room".
- **Work-life balance.** Increasingly individuals appreciate flexibility to help them juggle their work and personal responsibilities.
- **Recognition.** Recognition and constructive feedback from bosses and peers gives talented people "a real energy boost".

It seems safe to surmise that talented people are still driven by the same emotional and transactional needs when they are involved in a merger or acquisition and that these needs are probably heightened. The fluid state of a new business combination can offer many opportunities to motivate talented individuals by giving them various challenges. For example, they can be assigned to temporary projects or integration teams. They can be offered secondments to different areas of the business to learn new skills or disseminate skills and knowledge. They can be stretched by being matched with jobs that they are not yet equipped for, requiring them to grow on the job. This could include cross-functional moves, a transfer to an unfamiliar business unit, or a job involving profit and loss responsibility.

Just as important is ensuring that high-potential people are given personal attention by senior people, especially when they are waiting to be assigned a role. These individuals can be mentored and coached, even on an informal basis. Some companies take a more organised approach and actively track the people it is important to retain. Lucent Technologies closely monitors employee retention in every acquisition. Mary Jane Raymond, Lucent's merger integration vice-president, told The Conference Board:

> We ... monitor new hires and losses in every one of our weekly integration meetings after the announcement. We discuss the losses, the reasons, the efforts to keep the people (discussion of opportunities, financial packages, equity, "getting to know Lucent" talk, etc) and what we may need to do differently with the next person. The new hires and losses are reviewed with senior management every two weeks.

After the first few months of the acquisition, responsibility for attracting and retaining talented people is given to the new management team. Information about this area of the business is shared with the integration team, which has monthly meetings with the management team.

Development and training
Co-operation also entails helping people to co-operate by supporting them and equipping them to change their working practices. Training and development initiatives can play an important role during the period between announcement and closure and in the post-combination stage. Many companies use such forums to create "open spaces", where

employees have the opportunity to discuss their personal concerns and to begin to work out how they might need to adjust. Change-management sessions also help employees understand how individuals and organisations typically react to change.

Also valuable are development sessions aimed at getting management to work more as a team. In companies where managers are divided by disagreements about strategy and turf fighting, skilled mediators are used to help teams work through their differences. Messrs Marks and Mirvis[15] discuss how creating transparent decision-making processes and "political maps" helped to diffuse the managerial disputes that marred computer manufacturer IBM's acquisition of Lotus. "Transition" teams were required to reveal the logic and basis of their integration proposals by electronically recording their databases, analysis and work plans. This information was available to other teams so that they could question or challenge the proposals. Teams were also required to prepare political maps, analysing what was at stake for various stakeholders in the combination. The acquired management teams also made political maps, showing how different functions in IBM might potentially be affected by integration plans and identifying which individuals might be influenced to support the proposals. Messrs Marks and Mirvis believe that internal politics can be managed:

> We find that persistent and serious pressure to create value
> helps to keep political forces under control. Conflicts of interest
> do not vanish, but they do become manageable. At the same
> time, success also comes from selecting strategies that are
> politically feasible.

A two-sided thing

Another aspect of co-operation is that it needs to be mutual. Managers of a newly combined business cannot expect their staff simply to do what they are told – this would require their capitulation rather than their co-operation. Instead, they must be willing to listen to the views of employees and, whenever possible, negotiate a compromise. This demonstrates to staff that the new business is based on partnership, flexibility and mutual respect. For example, one acquirer discovered that its acquired staff were not satisfied with meeting human-resources staff from their new parent company, but expected a personal letter from the group CEO, inviting them to join the business. An Italian employee returned his letter, complaining it was too cold and distant, and refused to talk further until he received a warmer version. The acquired company was somewhat surprised by these reactions but acquiesced because it wanted to preserve the entrepreneurial culture of the acquired business.

Collaboration

Once there is a foundation of co-operation, it is possible to begin the task of encouraging people to contribute intellectually and emotionally to the emerging business.

In its simplest and most practical sense, collaboration hinges on:

- helping people to create personal networks across the new business so that knowledge and learning can be shared;
- physically bringing people together so that they can energise each other – and allowing them time to do this;
- accepting that cultural clashes are inevitable but can be used as opportunities to explore differences and help a new culture to emerge.

The pace of change can be so rapid during the integration phase that personal networks are disrupted or even lost entirely. This can impede the sharing of knowledge and learning across different parts of the organisation. Employees who rely on such networks to be effective in their roles also feel that they have lost a degree of competency at a time when they need to perform to their maximum ability. It is therefore in everyone's interest to find ways of reconnecting informal networks. Electronic communication can be invaluable. Glaxo Wellcome Inc, a subsidiary of Glaxo Wellcome, developed a website that gave up-to-date information about who was who and who worked for whom in the newly combined business. Ms Davis comments:

> Up to that point, it was not clear at all and there weren't any company charts that made any sense, and certainly they weren't being distributed. So we were able to use technology to which everybody in the company had access to start to illustrate the organisation as it was taking shape.[16]

Another solution is to bring together different groups of people (including external stakeholders such as customers and suppliers) in different forums. These gatherings should be run by skilled facilitators who are able to create a balance between structure and freedom. Discussions can be built around specific business issues, problems and opportunities. Groups can aim to improve, redesign or dramatically re-engineer processes, services and products. Discussions can be structured, or participants can be encouraged to brainstorm and express any idea, however bizarre or impractical.

However, collaboration also depends on people having time and space to work together and consider new possibilities – precious commodities in the hectic environment of an M&A. Gordon Dawes, UK director at GlaxoSmithKline, declares:

> The biggest barrier to innovation is simply enormous workloads. It is extraordinarily difficult to think about new ideas for the future when the immediate pressures of merging force you to concentrate on the here and now.

Mr Dawes says that one practical step is to make it as easy as possible for employees to express their ideas and suggestions. Simple devices such as graffiti boards and cards on tables in staff canteens enable people to note down their ideas, anonymously if they wish.

Taking people away from their jobs for a few days is another way of creating room for collaboration. AstraZeneca, a merged Swedish/British pharmaceuticals company, rolled out a global leadership programme for all its employees once the immediate transition was completed. Tony Bloxham, then UK vice-president (human resources), describes this:

> [It is a] dialogue process, giving everyone the opportunity to discuss what this value really means for them individually and for the new business. During the first module, everyone has the opportunity to examine how to do things differently and be more effective. We are saying that innovation is about giving people the freedom to contribute and push out the boundaries. Nothing is off bounds; there are no rules or regulations. This has been very motivating and we have lost very little of our talent base.[17]

Many companies also use existing networks and forums. At Zeneca, a series of "Creativity, Innovation and Learning" workshops continued during the run-up to the merger in 1999. These events drew people from all parts of the business to review innovations developed by employees that had delivered tangible benefits to the company. Employees analysed the role that individual leadership, as well as openness and honesty, played in helping to turn innovative ideas into successful innovations.

Louise Craigen, a workshop designer, says that this was a helpful way of emphasising the continued importance of creativity and innovation. At a time when merging workforces often become introspective and anxious, many of Zeneca's workshop delegates agreed to form an informal innovation network to share experiences, learning and examples of innovative solutions to business issues.

Collaboration also depends on employees feeling sure that they will receive recognition for their efforts. During M&A workshops at Roffey Park Institute, a pharmaceuticals manager supplied the following insight:

> During the merger, people buried their "babies". They felt that
> their previous track record had been negated by the merger.
> They felt like new recruits, forced to re-establish their
> credibility. Many good practices and new ideas went
> underground for a while. Some high-fliers were lost in the first
> few months because the company failed to "stroke" them
> enough.

Smoothing friction

Any form of joint working is valuable during M&As, but this will almost certainly involve cultural friction. As groups of people tackle real business issues, they will encounter countless examples of how the combining organisations speak a different language and codify their experiences. Behind every differing perception will be an implicit set of values that leads employees to think unconsciously that their way of working is "better".

For example, some months into its acquisition of DowBrands, SC Johnson, a producer of household and consumer products, experienced difficulty in achieving a synthesis between its marketing and distribution expertise and DowBrands's skill in product technology and engineering. SC Johnson told The Conference Board how it gathered data on cultural differences using a culture integration survey instrument. It then held a "building the bridge" meeting, where employees explored each company's approach to achievement, approval, avoiding conflict, risk aversion, centralisation/hierarchy, conventionality, control and competition. This opportunity to explore and express their different values led both organisations to accept that their capabilities were complementary and that they needed to change some of their attitudes and working practices in order to progress.

Cultural friction during integration is much better understood, and many cultural specialists now work with companies to help them resolve cultural differences. A starting point is for each company to understand its own culture before analysing whether the two companies' cultural values and working styles are complementary or conflicting. Cultural assessment tools help identify various manifestations of culture and how these affect people's attitudes towards such things as decision-making, power and managerial styles.

But it is important to keep strict control over costs as these can spiral in large complicated mergers, warns PricewaterhouseCoopers, as a result of its own experience when Price Waterhouse merged with Coopers & Lybrand. David Hadfield, the partner responsible for integrating the two firms during 1998, says:

> A big lesson for us was to avoid growing costs during integration. It happens easily. We were merging together almost 150,000 employees across 150 different countries. As we appointed new managers, our costs rapidly rose as those managers, acting out of the best intentions, took their people away from their work and got them together in order to help them become multicultural, global teams. As people worked on integration, the number of teams, activities and task-forces spiralled.
>
> We realised we needed to control our costs by simply doing less. We also told our people that it was legitimate for them to get together if they were a global team performing client work. If it was an internal project, people should not get together so frequently.

Commitment

People become committed to a merger when they believe:

- it is built on a sound strategy;
- it offers personal benefits in terms of financial incentives and career opportunities;

■ it meets their emotional needs;
■ the new business offers something unique that cannot be replicated in the separate businesses.

The last factor represents for employees the "added value" of any M&A or a winning "employee value proposition". To get the best from people, you must stimulate their emotions and energies and convince them that the pain and disruption is worthwhile. Once a M&A's unique employee value proposition has been articulated, it can become a strong unifying factor during integration, helping to energise and motivate everyone.

The unifying "big idea" is unique to each M&A. It may be the combination's brand that stirs people's loyalty and commitment, or it may be a sense that the combination has a unique method of working. Ogilvy & Mather, and advertising agency, is in this category. All of its acquisitions are made with the aim of supporting its commitment to give "360-degree branding" to its clients – an approach that requires different agencies within the group to pool their creativity and expertise in order to deliver an integrated range of marketing and public relations services to clients.

Cisco is convinced that its ability to offer exciting new opportunities to newcomers is the main reason for its impressive record of retaining the entrepreneurial founders of the companies it acquires. Says one such former owner/manager:

> What I really love about this place is the context of ideas. Because we have people from different companies, there are different approaches to solving problems. That creates an atmosphere of excitement that even the best small company cannot duplicate.

Although this manager misses the control of running an independent business, he says: "What Cisco's global marketing capacity has given me instead is the chance to kick our products through the roof."

"Big ideas" help capture people's imaginations, but commitment also rests on the day-to-day experience of working in the new business. Energy and creative thought can dissipate quickly if there is a stolid lump of managers and team leaders who discourage people from making waves or taking risks. Any effort to build a more capable business must therefore include recognition of the critical role that managers and team leaders – the electrons who move around the nucleus – play in determining whether it is business as usual or business as unusual.

8 Stirring the electrons: the role of managers and team leaders

THOSE IN CHARGE of the integration process may be setting off all sorts of reactions in the nucleus of the combining organisations, but surrounding their activities are countless electrons – the managers responsible for the day-to-day running of the business. The contribution these people can make in helping a newly combined business find its feet and get off to a good start is often overlooked. Despite all the changes and distractions, it is their responsibility to keep business activities on track. They must deal with high levels of disruption. Overseeing redundancies and new appointments, they have the difficult task of rebuilding their operational teams and helping the people in them adjust and eventually thrive in the emerging business. These individuals are also experiencing personal and professional changes, and may themselves to a greater or lesser degree need support and help during the transition.

The day-to-day role of managers is often neglected when businesses have merged for a number of reasons. Senior managers are frequently preoccupied with formulating strategy and communicating progress to, for example, investors and analysts. When they do turn their attention to internal matters, it often centres on designing the integration plan and governance structure, as well as setting and monitoring performance goals. Integration teams are working at a frenetic pace to eliminate duplications and create shared processes and activities. The day-to-day manager, in contrast, seems a small cog in a fast-moving, giant wheel.

Operational managers may not formulate strategy or effect dramatic business transformation, but their role is essential. Like electrons, their movement and activity has the potential to alter the atomic "reactivity" of the emerging business. They are the "reality" makers, the people in the organisation who have the opportunity to transform lofty statements about collaboration and synergy into constructive, day-to-day experiences of successful joint working. Their job is to "mind the gap" between policy and working practices so that in the absence of formalised processes and structures, employees can remain sane and whole, and even begin to flourish in the new environment. They are also uniquely positioned to build trust among employees by ensuring that difficult changes are implemented as professionally and humanely as possible. The opposite is also true. Line managers who channel all their efforts into preserving or promoting their own careers at the expense of those around them have a corrosive effect on their employees and will speedily dissolve any goodwill or openness to change.

This chapter is based on off-the-record interviews with managers and staff from a number of companies, as well as insights gathered from a series of workshops on merger management held by Roffey Park Institute in the UK between 1997 and 2000, which resulted in a merger "checklist" for line managers.[1] These discussions strongly suggest that employees attach much greater importance to what their immediate boss says and does than to various promises and "visionary" statements issued by merger teams.

The following sections explore the practical steps that operational managers can take to help their teams adjust to their new circumstances and adopt more collaborative and creative working practices. Much of the discussion rests on the premise that human-resources staff will support line managers in two principal ways: by working with them to handle their staffing challenges with as much professionalism as possible; and providing personal support at a time when they may well feel isolated and overstretched.

Co-ordination: helping people understand where they fit

Previous chapters point out that the shock caused by a merger announcement is exacerbated when companies fail to inform employees quickly of what is likely to happen to them during the next few weeks and months. Employees left in limbo can either quit or become one of the "walking wounded". The round of redundancies and job transfers that typically occur during the first three months or so of an M&A also causes merger shock.

Line managers must somehow keep their teams focused and performing during a time of great uncertainty, especially in the interim period between announcement and completion. Their first task is to prevent their team from sliding into introspection, depression and endless, mainly negative, speculation about the forthcoming changeover. Although they may know as little as those who report to them, line managers can aim to listen and learn by doing the following.

Work to create a climate of openness

Line managers can use the "lull before the storm" to build up their staff and prepare them for change. Employees are often positive and open at this stage and may therefore be more prepared to express their views and concerns. For example, a middle manager who worked on her organisation's alliance development team, comments:

> When I first heard about the merger and how it would affect our unit, I felt very excited. When we went away for half a day to discuss the merger, I genuinely felt that I would rather have a lesser role in a new improved unit than be in a stronger position in a weaker unit. I had been frustrated for some time with the rivalry between different groups and the unwillingness to learn from one another.

Positive and negative viewpoints need to be heard. The first step is to listen, rather than to preach the official message about the combination's supposed benefits. Line managers can learn about their staff's reaction to the announcement by asking open-ended questions about their perceptions of the pluses and minuses of the proposed new arrangement.

Some interesting and surprising information may come to light if people are asked how they view the firm they are merging with. For example, given the increase of mergers within the same industry sector, employees often have direct experience of the firm they are joining – some may even have worked for it in the past. This discussion may yield valuable information about the other company's culture and style of working. When Lloyds TSB acquired Scottish Widows, for example, according to a software engineer in the information technology unit, many of the employees in the unit had strong preconceptions about Scottish Widows's software and IT processes and were convinced that Lloyds TSB's "superior" approaches would be introduced in the acquisition. Lloyds TSB's decision to adopt Scottish Widows's software in one important process (a work-flow system) seemed inexplicable to many of its own staff and made collaboration between the two companies' IT departments very difficult.

Line managers can help their staff recognise their own change-management skills by discussing situations in the past where they have managed a difficult transition – perhaps a house move or the birth of a baby. Some people may have actual experience of a merger or acquisition and be able to provide some valuable insights and advice. This can also be the opportunity to design just-in-time training and development (see next page).

Just-in-time M&A training

In autumn 1999, a British company was about to be acquired by a large international group that had only limited experience in merger integration and had thus far rejected offers of help from the acquired company's human-resources director and team. The HR team decided to do all that it could to prepare its staff for the changeover before legal closure. It used up its remaining budget on training and development initiatives build around the following goals.

- Build an organisational capability to cope with an acquisition experience.
- Enhance the organisation's "change capability".
- Promote a positive perception of the forthcoming integration process.
- Nurture cross-functional collaboration.

The team quickly offered managers and employees the following support.

- A brief but provocative merger handbook produced by an American consultancy for all senior managers.
- A two-hour communication session over three weeks for all managers, after which they received a "survival" guide, which gave them an overview of M&As and suggestions on how to help their staff.
- A one-day workshop for managers, looking at handling change.
- Two one-week leadership programmes for all operational managers, incorporating elements of change management and positive thinking.

The company's one-day workshop looked at change-management competencies such as flexibility, innovation, risk tolerance and stress tolerance, and helped managers understand how individuals and organisations react to change. The training and development team fed into the workshop a simple employee attitude survey that it conducted to help gauge people's responses to the acquisition announcement. The workshop also examined strategies for preventing the typical dip in performance immediately after an M&A. It examined why and how people resist change. As a final aid to managing personal change, participants underwent psychometric tests to help them understand their own working styles and preferences.

Feedback about the workshop was extremely positive, with participants indicating that the two most useful subjects were managing change and managing resistance.

These discussions can help "sound the emotional barometer" by encouraging people to talk about negative experiences of M&As that may be colouring their reaction. Line managers can begin to pinpoint the issues that may become obstacles to change during the immediate transition. It is valuable if they pass on these general insights to the integration or human-resources team.

Combat "them versus us" thinking

Various M&A studies already mentioned discussed the tendency among employees to distrust the firm they are merging with on account of the exaggerated or distorted perspectives they have of the way it operates. One way of combating "demon mythologising" is to provide staff with more objective information. For example:

- circulate newspaper articles that analyse the deal;
- surf the Internet and company websites to help build up a profile of the other business – this information can help the team begin to think about how the combining organisations might work together;
- use personal networks to find out about counterparts in the partner business and contact them, ideally through e-mail, to begin building relationships.

Chaperone "first dates"

Companies usually take great care in preparing for the first round of meetings between senior managers and employees. Much less attention is given to the interactions taking place between managers and functional specialists of the combining organisations. Employee focus groups suggest that these meetings are highly sensitive and that managers and specialist staff, who are in effect "ambassadors", may not realise how easily they can cause offence or create misconceptions about their own organisations. Line managers should prepare their staff by:

- ensuring that they are adequately briefed about the nature of the meeting. For example, is the aim to gather information, share information or simply network with counterparts?
- alerting them to their role as ambassadors and stressing that if they appear arrogant or judgmental they will cause resentment;
- emphasising that the M&A is a partnership and that their behaviour and terminology should reflect this;

- helping them avoid making assumptions about the nature and structure of the combination. For example, it is easy for the staff of the acquiring company to assume that their processes, not those of the acquired business, will be adopted.
- paying attention to the social niceties of knowing the correct names, titles, spelling, qualifications, track records (and any another other information they can get their hands on) of their counterparts. This can make a big difference in showing how much people matter to the business.

New terms and conditions

As the details of the transition emerge, managers should be provided with as much information as possible about changes in terms and conditions. Although communication processes are often handled by the human-resources function, especially in smaller companies, line managers still play an important role by speaking on behalf of their team and filtering questions and answers. Given the potentially explosive nature of remuneration, managers can also provide invaluable feedback about their team's reactions to the changed terms and conditions.

Handling new appointments

Those that have been involved in successful M&As will often emphasise the benefits of involving line managers and team leaders in decisions about new appointments, rather than leaving this in the hands of an integration team or a centralised human-resources function. As one line manager working for an international car manufacturing company argues:

> Bosses must be involved in the hiring of their subordinates or the new organisation won't work. This takes time and causes tension, but it is a vital part of the merger process.

If they are not part of the decision-making process, line managers will be less well equipped to deal with the inevitable rumours and political speculation that follow each round of new appointments. One employee who worked for an organisation supplying community-care services speaks of her cynicism about the appointment process:

> The rhetoric didn't match up with the reality. It appeared as though a lot of people were being stitched up. A lot of good

people who didn't "talk the talk" were pushed aside. The same group of people, the ones who were willing to play politics, were "cosying" up to senior managers and getting the key roles. In the end, it felt like nothing had changed except people's titles. We lost many good people during the transition because their way of working was not being valued. Some were leaving their jobs, but others were opting out psychologically.

To prevent such disillusionment, managers need to take the following steps (liaising closely with human resources).

- Ensure that everyone understands the selection criteria and the selection process itself.
- Document processes and be ready to justify any decisions.
- Maintain high professional standards. Don't take shortcuts, even though the pressure to build a new team is intense.
- Keep employees informed. If the process stalls or is delayed for some reason, communicate this quickly and give firm details about when selection procedures will restart.
- Reassure people about the fairness of decisions by gathering as much information as possible about their experiences, past achievements and track record. In some cases, the combining organisations may not have the same quality and depth of information about their employees' experiences and capabilities. In order to make the best decision and avoid bias towards one organisation's candidates, use personal networks to supplement information about job candidates.
- Resist the temptation to fudge decisions. To grow the revenue of the combined business, it is essential to build capable teams as soon as possible. Making decisions based on internal politics may yield short-term advantages but could cause serious problems in the long term.

Handling redundancies

During the immediate post-acquisition stage, line managers are likely to handle redundancies, probably alongside human-resources staff. It is essential that people leaving the company are treated with consideration and respect, both for their own sake and as a way of reassuring survivors that the combining organisations care about their staff. Delegating this unpleasant task is a mistake, as most people expect to hear the news from their immediate boss, not a more senior person or someone from the human-resources department.

Line managers should ensure that they are prepared for redundancy meetings. Ideally, they should have received training in how to handle redundancies, but there may not be enough time available before the redundancy programme begins. Practical advice is supplied by Drake Beam Morin (DBM), an "outplacement" specialist that has offices in 39 countries. DBM recommends the following procedures for managers.

- Prepare materials so you can explain the reasons and ensure that you have severance information in writing, including formal notification, details of salary continuation or severance period, benefits and any further support such as careers counselling.
- Prepare the message by writing down what information must be communicated.
- Arrange the next steps, such as meetings with human-resources staff, and think through details, such as when individuals should clear their desks and what should be done with company cars and personal belongings.
- Prepare emotionally. Breaking the news of redundancy is difficult and you must remember that you are not personally responsible. Talking over the meeting beforehand with a colleague or HR specialist can be helpful.
- Anticipate how the person will react. Research by DBM reveals that there are five typical reactions to redundancy.
  - Anticipation. Individuals have been aware of the possibility, and although they may have dreaded the event, they are in some ways relieved. They are generally composed during the redundancy meeting and are able to focus on practical matters.
  - Disbelief. Individuals are shocked and cannot easily conduct a sensible conversation. They may plead for the decision to be reversed, or go into a state of denial and try to terminate the meeting and return to their offices.
  - Escape. Individuals simply want to escape and may storm out of the meeting before receiving any severance details.
  - Euphoria. Individuals try to please their boss and make the situation less difficult by being amenable and positive.
  - Violence. This is the least common reaction. Although individuals feel angry, they usually resort to screaming and swearing rather than physical violence.

Jane Rothwell, principal consultant at Meridian Consultancy, a London-based firm that works with many financial services companies, stresses the importance of handling redundancies well:

> *If employees feel they were treated fairly and the managers were well prepared, had the documentation to hand and treated them as human beings, they should leave the company with few hard feelings. For the staff remaining in the company, if they see departing employees treated with respect ... then they know their company is one that values people.*

She advises managers to choose a neutral place for the meeting, preferably away from the individual's working area, where the news can be given privately and without interruption. She suggests arranging another meeting a couple of days later to go over the same information when the individual is calmer. The rest of the team and department need to know as soon as possible, before rumours circulate. Use the announcement to acknowledge the individual's achievements and contribution. Make a point of being accessible to remaining staff, some of whom may feel upset, anxious or guilty about staying, and be willing reassure them about their own future with the company.

Dealing with redundancies requires line managers to be both intuitive and well organised. As well as ensuring that the leavers are treated with consideration, managers must acknowledge the impact that this will have on the remaining team members. They must then judge when the team is ready to move forward. Only then can the manager reiterate the message of future business growth and the prime objectives of the combination as a means of refocusing the team.

Co-operation

Overcoming resistance to change

It is easy to overlook the fact that M&As of all kinds generate waves of emotion throughout the organisation as employees experience personal and work changes. The role of senior managers is to provide direction and vision during this turbulent time. However, it is the line manager or team leader who must deal with the immediate human fallout. There is no avoiding this task, as unresolved issues and emotions will simply fester. Even worse, these reactions can be incorporated into the "collective memory" of the organisation, becoming a lodestar for negative feelings of resentment, bitterness and cynicism. When the next merger or

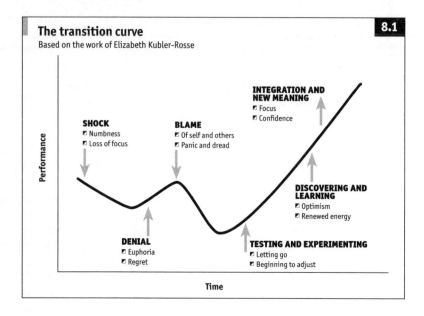

The transition curve   **8.1**
Based on the work of Elizabeth Kubler-Rosse

acquisition comes along, the attitudes of surviving employees are adversely coloured by their past experiences.

Any standard M&A or change-management guide discusses how individuals undergo a series of emotional responses to change. The transition curve, developed by Elizabeth Kubler-Rosse, remains the standard model for explaining the typical response to change. The stages people go through are illustrated in Chart 8.1.

Managers need to understand these stages and help employees work through their reactions as quickly as possible so that the whole team can become capable of learning through collaborating. Giving people support and the opportunity to voice their views and feelings is one way of helping them move on. Another is small celebrations, for example, of past events and achievements, or of current achievements such as reaching an important team milestone.

Line managers act as important "change barometers" when they supply feedback about their team's ability to deal with different waves of change. Failure to recognise where teams are on the transition curve can lead to a mistaken assumption that individuals or teams are resisting change. Integration managers, and senior managers in particular, can become out of touch with how different teams and departments are responding to the transition and may appear insensitive, or they may try to initiate another series of changes before people are ready.

Employees of a company that had a strong reputation and a set of cherished values and traditions found the experience of being bought by a more commercially oriented conglomerate difficult to accept. The human-resources director discovered that the acquiring company assumed that its latest acquisition was "preparing for battle" rather than simply grappling with change. She worked with a number of people within her organisation to prepare a briefing document for the new parent company. A customised transition curve was used, profiling four phases of resistance and illustrated by comments from anonymous employees. These stages are as follows.

- ◪ Betrayal: "we've been hung out to dry"; "their negotiators knew what they were doing better than ours"; "our management team have all gone to ground" and "they got their golden wheelbarrows"; "they think we're just a sleepy little business".
- ◪ Denial: "There is no point me trying as I can't influence anything"; "I'm just keeping my head down and carrying on"; "they'll soon realise we're better than them in many respects".
- ◪ Identity crisis: "I don't know what is expected"; "I haven't the knowledge for this"; "I have no career now".
- ◪ Search for solutions: "I'm trying to get my voice heard"; "I've changed how I do things to match their expectations".

As well as trying to get the parent company to understand these stages of adjustment and the various issues concerning employees, the HR director also explained that different waves of "resistance" were affecting senior managers, line managers and employees because of the timing of various changes. She comments:

> Because their situations are resolved first, senior managers can become frustrated with management and employees, who may still be working through the earlier stages of betrayal and denial. Employees can then feel that their senior managers don't care about them. If this situation is not recognised, it can destabilise the whole organisation.

Line managers also need to look out for "survivor sickness" among any employees whose jobs were on the line for a time and who witnessed redundancies among their colleagues. Mitchell Lee Marks and

Paul Mirvis, two M&A experts, coined this memorable phrase.[2] They argue that survivors settle into three different mindsets, which can become destructive over time.

- The ready: people who have achieved the hoped for job change or promotion and who are thus full of energy and enthusiasm. This commendable state of mind can, however, tip into aggressive and superior behaviour.
- The wanting: people who did not receive the job they wanted or who were effectively demoted. They often become angry and depressed, but with support and encouragement, they might eventually adjust to their changed circumstances.
- The wrung out: people who remain in the same job but whose work environment has changed. They often become equally frustrated by the similarities and differences of their work life. Some may work through these frustrations and accept their lot; others may become demotivated and lose any sense of purpose and direction.

There is a limit to what line managers can do to help their teams adjust to changes. They should:

- accept that they cannot resolve people's concern or issues – they can, however, listen to them, acknowledge their importance and communicate them to integration teams or senior managers;
- try not to make rash promises or guarantees to salve people's feelings – broken promises only heighten feelings of betrayal;
- be honest and as open as possible, especially about the extent and limit of their information;
- avoid the mistake of trying to protect staff by delaying communicating bad news or minimising its implications – this will only annoy people and lessen their confidence in the reliability and trustworthiness of their manager;
- provide opportunities for people to express negative views and emotions, and let them express them without feeling pressurised to rush in with consolation, advice or platitudes.

Encouraging intellectual buy-in

Intellectual buy-in is easier to achieve than emotional buy-in. Managers should provide opportunities for their teams to discuss the details of the

M&A. Official announcements can be followed by team meetings to discuss and clarify the new information, before exploring the implications for the team itself. This can be a valuable opportunity for less outgoing employees to voice their opinions.

If line managers cannot persuade resistant people to articulate their true feelings, they may become powerful, if silent, obstacles to change. Alyson Morley, a former manager at a British government agency that merged with another during 2000, speaks of this problem:

> We adopted a new business excellence model but the people who were the unhappiest with the concepts tended to say nothing. They just opted out of the process of discussion. They were unhappy and disenchanted, but they said nothing. When the unit put it to senior managers that it was difficult to express dissatisfaction, they decided to ask various questions in an employee satisfaction survey. Although the survey was anonymous, respondents had to give their grade and line manager. Everyone felt that it would be easy to be identified, so the disaffected people still didn't fill in the questionnaire.

Line managers should encourage their staff to exploit fully any communication processes that have been created during the transition period. The team should develop its own communication plan, identifying those it wishes to influence – perhaps a departmental head, integration manager or executive, or even external opinion formers such as analysts, journalists and lobbyists.

To encourage intellectual buy-in, managers should:

- repeat important messages, especially about the benefits of the combination – this helps prevent staff being overwhelmed by details and losing the bigger picture;
- anticipate how their teams will react to the latest merger announcement and prepare their own question-and-answer presentation;
- supplement any gaps in official announcements by networking with other managers to discover what is happening, or to help resolve ambiguities or confusions in work tasks and processes;
- prepare for negative feeling among teams after each formal announcement and recognise people's need for fresh reassurance.

Engaging talented individuals

Line managers and team leaders are well positioned to identify and track talented individuals within their units and teams. Unlike a centralised team that is responsible for the recruitment and retention of high-fliers, managers have the opportunity to maintain close working relationships with these individuals. They can encourage them and reassure them about their future, especially when they feel overlooked by more senior managers or are frustrated by the lack of opportunities to contribute their ideas.

Personal encouragement can make a significant difference to talented employees. For example, a middle manager at Zurich, an insurance company, which merged with British American Financial Services in 1998, says that the support of his line manager prevented him from leaving during the long period, approximately 12 months, between the merger announcement and completion. His department ran out of work and many people sat around for months simply reading and chatting. The manager felt deeply frustrated and also guilty about receiving a good salary for no significant effort:

> I was also ambitious and I felt convinced that I could work at a higher level and that the merger could well provide me with an opportunity to do so.

Unfortunately, Zurich could not begin any integration activities until the merger was completed. The manager says that his boss helped him keep motivated during that time:

> He was an excellent manager of people. I knew that he cared about what happened to me and that he particularly wanted to help those people who were willing to be proactive, rather than sitting around assuming that the company owed them a living.

The manager had regular, informal meetings with his boss where they discussed how he could raise his profile within Zurich and position himself to take advantage of any opportunities offered by the merger.

> He boosted my confidence, which I was beginning to lose, by telling me that I was capable, that I did have the potential to operate at a more senior level, and that I needed to hang in until the merger went through.

His boss's advice and encouragement helped the manager invent various projects that enabled him to network with other departments and meet other "like-minded individuals". He was eventually seconded to an integration team and at the end of the process was promoted to a senior management post.

Collaboration

For many line managers, collaboration can appear to be an added luxury at a time when they are under pressure to achieve exacting, short-term performance targets. They therefore do not commit time and energy to creating opportunities to collaborate within newly formed teams, or across various functions and divisions. Their tendency to resort to more familiar ways of working can, unfortunately, appear to endorse the message that the old ways are the best ways.

A manager at a telecommunications company, for example, says that despite the fact that senior managers appeared to be genuinely committed to encouraging new ways of working in the merged business, line managers appeared more interested in promoting their protégés than innovative individuals. She declares:

> I was naive at the start of the merger, along with a number of my colleagues. Rather than promoting themselves, the good people initially tried to work constructively to get the merger to succeed. I learnt a bitter lesson that during a merger the people with good ideas don't receive credit for them. One manager who was particularly good at partnership working, and who was approachable and open to good ideas, had to reapply for her job. Even though everybody believed she was the most capable candidate, she failed to be reappointed. We all felt that the person who filled her position was simply better at promoting himself to senior managers. There was a real loss of trust during that time. People knew that they were supposed to be collaborative and constructive, but they felt that their managers wouldn't give them any credit for sharing their ideas.
>
> This culture of distrust was exacerbated by the fact that we all had to reapply for our positions and so we felt that we were in competition with each other. People knew their job was on the line and this created a blame culture. I don't see how you can seek to reduce staff numbers and tell them at the

*same time that they must work together to improve the
business and find optimal ways of working together.*

*In this climate, nobody was willing to learn from mistakes –
there was no recognition that innovation entails risk. The same
mistakes kept being made months after the merger because
people were unwilling to explore the underlying reasons. I
eventually opted for voluntary redundancy because I felt we
weren't making the best of people's skills and abilities in our
unit. Everyone was ploughing their own furrow with no real
understanding of what other people were doing. There was no
synergy or collaboration.*

If collaboration is to become a reality, line managers must be strongly
convinced of the need to try new ways of working. Senior managers
need to spend time with more junior managers to explore how and why
they should work differently. It should also be appreciated that collaboration is complex, difficult to achieve and entails a degree of risk for line
managers, many of whom may already feel insecure about their career
prospects in the new business. The issue of failure needs to be explored
– will managers be penalised if they make mistakes? How will the
organisation ensure that they and their teams receive credit for collaborative working, especially if their contribution is in the form of inputs
that are difficult to quantify, such as knowledge, market intelligence or
business contacts? Managers will also need to know whether aspects of
their appraisal will explore collaborative working, or whether it will still
be based on traditional performance measures.

Sharing knowledge and learning

The previous chapter emphasised that collaboration entails sharing
knowledge and learning. Line managers and team leaders, especially
technical specialists, have an important role as "knowledge brokers"
during the transition. Research into "knowledge creation" within businesses is pointing increasingly to the role that individuals play. For
example, Ikujiro Nonaka,[3] an adjunct professor at the School of Knowledge Science, Japan Advanced Institute of Science and Technology,
argues that knowledge creation is achieved through an upward spiral
rather than a top-down process. Knowledge spirals up the organisation
as individuals interact with each other. Knowledge starts at the individual level, moves to the group level and then to the corporate level. These
interactions or connections are crucial for knowledge acquisition.

Andrew Inkpen, an academic, develops this concept[4] and says that the formation of such knowledge connections are essential for corporate learning. There must be connections at each organisational level, where managers can share their observations and experiences. These connections occur through both formal and informal relationships among individuals and groups. Mr Inkpen explains:

Internal managerial relationships facilitate the sharing and communication of new knowledge and provide a basis for transforming individual knowledge to organisational knowledge.

Without knowledge, connections that are "consciously managed ... individual knowledge, which is inherently fragile ... may be ignored or viewed as irrelevant". Mr Inkpen suggests that managers can use the following to encourage knowledge creation.

- Temporary transfers of talented individuals, which help the transfer of tacit knowledge.
- Internal workshops looking at specific topics, where explicit and tacit knowledge can be exchanged.
- Visits to different parts of organisation, or along the stages of a work process or activity, to understand better how people work.

Discussions with managers who work across functions or with a variety of strategic partners reveal that collaborative working can be encouraged in a number of ways. For example, an alliance team leader describes the tactics he used to get employees from several different organisations to work on a joint project.[5] He supplies the following checklist.

- **Openness.** "As team leader, I tell people straight out what is in it for them. It is necessary to overcome any suspicions and barriers by being very open. It is important to be up-front and to keep emphasising the benefits of working together. There can be no hidden agendas."
- **Gift bearing.** "This is very important. In order to make things happen and to help people loosen up, I have had to give something of tangible value. I took the plunge and contributed my own personal databank, containing labour-market statistics."

- **A sense of humour.** "A 'playful seriousness' is an effective way to help people work together and get something done ... I simply try to ensure that people enjoy meeting together."
- **Facilitation skills.** "You need to keep tight control of meetings, without imposing your view as team leader. You need to ensure that all the team members are contributing their views and ideas."
- **Professionalism.** "This is an important quality for every team leader. We all respect each other's capabilities."

Handling culture clashes

Senior managers can set the tone for the new business by defining and demonstrating a small number of significant values and behaviours, but it is line managers who are at the front line of any cultural battles.

Line managers must view cultural tension and conflict as an inevitable part of an M&A. They should work closely with human-resources specialists and perhaps receive training to improve their understanding of how culture is manifested in group and individual behaviour. They should be steered towards useful classifications of organisational cultures. For example, Roger Davis's model[6] of business styles is still widely used. He looks at differences in such areas as degree of risk-taking and attitudes to power and control. Consultants Roger Harrison and Herb Stokes[7] diagnose four different types of cultures: power-based, role-based, task/achievement-based and person/support-based. Terrence Deal and Alan Kennedy,[8] two cultural specialists, look at managerial behaviour, risk-taking and feedback and describe four different cultures, such as "the tough-guy macho" culture and the "process" or bureaucratic culture.

Wendy Hall, a management consultant, argues that managers need to understand the different cultures of the respective partners as the first step towards becoming "culturally literate".[9] The next step is to:

- analyse the strengths and weaknesses of these cultures;
- assess the opportunity for cultural synergy;
- exercise cultural flexibility;
- build in "cultural mediation" to resolve cultural misunderstanding.

Managers attending workshops at Roffey Park Institute came up with the following advice.

- Identify the tactics used by team members to preserve their own cultures – for example, automatically assuming that different ways of working are "wrong".
- Identify cultural "hot spots" – obvious differences in working practices that generate tension or conflict and which therefore need to be tackled immediately.
- Using an appropriate cultural model, get team members to explore the traits of their own cultures (or even subcultures) and ask them what was good or bad about these.
- Get the team to identify the cultural values or meanings that are important to them and which they would like to see continuing in the new business.
- Challenge team members to identify a set of values that everyone can commit to and use it as a foundation for working together.

Commitment

Interviews with employees caught up in mergers and acquisitions reveal time after time that their line managers had a profound influence on how well they survived the initial transition and how positively they regarded their new organisation. The bottom line is that employees set greater store on what their immediate boss says and does than on any promises or statements made by senior managers. A powerful cocktail can be created when the actions and behaviours of their line managers are aligned with the combination's business priorities and integration approach. Organisations ignore the potential contribution of line managers and project leaders at their peril.

Commitment is based on a person's decision to invest his or her talent in the organisation and to endorse its values or business mission. Line managers cannot force such commitment, but they can nurture it by building strong relationships with their staff and thereby strengthening their attachment to the organisation. Supplying support and direction can also be a lifeline for staff undergoing rapid and difficult change, enabling line managers to give the combination a "human face", which can be especially valuable when the new business's identity and brands are in a state of flux. None of this requires rocket science or MBA-style intellectual wizardry, simply common sense, a genuine concern about people and a willingness to consider other viewpoints. As one manager says, "you need to be a good manager – in spades".

9 Achieving fusion: releasing creative energy

The jury may still be out regarding the AOL Time Warner merger, but the launch of the first Harry Potter film in late 2001 was being hailed as the first real payback of the two companies' much-hyped merger the previous year.

The film has been a huge box-office success, and according to Richard Parsons, co-chief operating officer, in an interview with *The Economist*, Harry Potter is "the most successful franchise in the history of Warner Brothers ... up there with Star Wars – or maybe even bigger".

Mr Parsons argues that the Harry Potter franchise shows what a well-integrated media conglomerate can conjure up in the way of cross-promotional synergies. The film was made by Warner Brothers, AOL Time Warner's movie arm. The soundtrack was recorded by Atlantic Records, a label from the Warner Music Group. Advanced reviews appeared in *Time* magazine and *Entertainment Weekly*, both from the group's publishing division. And all the while, AOL websites have been promoting the film through games, competitions, sneak previews and advanced bookings.

You can bring a horse to water...

Would all this have occurred if the two halves of AOL Time Warner had remained separate? No, stresses Mr Parsons. The heads of the various divisions, notorious for running their own patch in Time Warner days, would not think about "synergies" as much as they do when they are forced to sit together every two weeks. Integration, says Mr Parsons, imposes creativity and encourages thinking in the group's interests.

The proof of the creative magic will become more conclusive when cross-company teams start to come up with, for example, multimedia franchises and products that are developed for as well as being simply disseminated on the screen, through CDs and on the Internet. Forcing people to sit together in the same room every two weeks does not mean that the human interaction that occurs will be creative or that if it is, it will be properly followed through.

In January 1997, Scottish Enterprise, a British government agency, conducted a two-year experiment before moving its staff into a new building. Four teams offering advice to small businesses worked in an open-plan office that offered "hot" desks that anyone could use, virtual communications and reflection areas.

After 18 months some benefits were observed. Staff used their time more effectively and the experiment overtly reduced "presenteeism", where team members judged each other on the hours they put in rather than on results. However, improvements in creativity and synergy were less obvious. People seemed to become more creative within their immediate work circle, but communication barriers among teams – particularly their ability to make linkages between their work or to consider how the methods used by other teams could be applied in their own areas – held back the progress that had been expected. Moreover, the notion that providing relaxing social areas would, of itself, foster a spontaneous sharing of knowledge and ideas did not prove true in practice. People shared ideas more readily with people whom they knew already but failed to do so with anyone new.

Individuals and innovation

At its most basic level, innovation is the systematic development, application and exploitation of new ideas. Ideas, although they may be shaped collectively, originate in individuals. As Ewen Bewley, European head of intellectual property at Nortel Networks, a telecoms company, comments: "Ideas are our lifeblood and they come from individuals, not processes or the application of new technology."

But individuals are, well, individual – and some are more individual than others. They respond to change in different ways and have agendas that do not always tie in neatly with those of their employer. An organisation has a right to expect that anyone who works for it undertakes to meet certain standards, but if it wants its staff to go an extra mile, it must give serious thought to the circumstances in which individuals are most likely to make the effort. Research by those studying innovation and those examining the "people" aspects of mergers and acquisitions at Roffey Park Institute in the UK suggests that when employees feel their future with the organisation is at risk, they are less willing to take risks and experiment and will display one of or both the following symptoms.

◪ Psychological withdrawal. The individual is unable to think or act creatively because of work-based stress. The most common sources of personal stress, as documented by Cary Cooper, BUPA professor of organisational psychology and health at Manchester

Chart 9.1 **What are the most common causes of stress?**

	% of respondents
Life events, eg, divorce, moving house, marriage	57
Increased workload caused by downsizing	56
Job insecurity	46
Rapid change	41
Long working hours	31
Difficulty in balancing home and work	31
Managers who have unrealistic expectations	29
Poor management	28
Changing skill requirements	28
Productivity/performance targets	23

Source: Cary Cooper, UMIST, 2000

School of Management (see Chart 9.1), include downsizing, job insecurity, rapid change and changing skill requirements. All of these are real or perceived common by-products of M&AS.

◼ Psychological work-to-rule. The individual is unphased by the insecurities and uncertainties of the merger but chooses to hold back his or her creative cards until the full personal consequences of the change become clearer. In the eyes of psychological work-to-rulers, their own creative ideas and insights are negotiable assets that will be auctioned off to the highest bidder or could be used to set up on their own.

Employees, according to the Roffey research, respond in these ways to any period of uncertainty or change, whether caused by recession, relocation, quality initiatives or shifts in strategic direction. But the intensity of the perceived change is exceptionally high in the case of mergers, and the ability of professional and managerial staff to tap into the rumour mill will be correspondingly fine-tuned.

What this means in practice

If the three "people" imperatives of successful mergers – co-ordination, co-operation and collaboration – are factored into what is known about how innovative capabilities are affected by sudden change or career insecurity, the following additional priorities emerge.

Stage one: co-ordination – helping people to see where they fit in
Maintaining "business as usual" reassurances is likely to be seen by the
staff you most want to keep as an insult to their intelligence. The first
rumour of merger talk will have put their minds at red alert. But the
smartest and most valuable people will also see the process not as a
threat but as an opportunity to further their careers. The most valuable
card they can put on the table is also the least quantifiable: their creativity, and through it the added value they bring to their job. If the organisation shows little sign of recognising their value, smart people will
draw their own conclusions and start looking for alternatives, if not in
deadly earnest at least as a way of hedging their bets. Once they start
looking, it is likely that they will find a new job – perhaps not immediately but after six months or a year when their contribution is most
needed.

This book argues that to prevent the loss of the organisation's creative capabilities, through either the physical loss of valuable knowledge workers or the loss of their intellectual engagement, measures
will need to be undertaken through formal human-resources or other
channels. However, the more subtle (and therefore more effective)
messages – reassurances that the person is valued and that he or she
has a future within the organisation – can be channelled through informal networks.

Maximum use should be made of "gatekeepers", managers who
through a small number of critical relationships link the various parts of
the business, and "pulsetakers", managers whose cross-functional
responsibilities cut across all hierarchies and whose web of relationships allows them to know what everyone in the organisation is thinking or feeling. Working in collaboration with the IBM Advanced
Business Unit, Karen Stephenson, a professor of management at the University of California at Los Angeles, has found that such individuals, the
people who shape the conversation in the corridors, often play a crucial
role in succession planning, influencing who stays and who goes during
periods of intense change.

Stage two: co-operation

This is the point at which, as Chapter 5 showed, the two organisations
set up integration teams and cross-functional project groups. To foster
and sustain innovation, these groups need not only to be made up of the
right people but also to work in a more creative fashion. Organisations
should seize the opportunity of "starting from zero" to establish ground

rules for the way in which these teams work that subsequently can be transferred to all work units.

Danah Zohar, a physicist turned management guru, points out that the origins of most management thinking lie in the Newtonian theories of science that dominated North American and European universities in the late 19th century. These taught that all things are simple, law-abiding and ultimately controllable. But at a time of constant change, when innovation is at a premium, a more useful foundation for management thought is that of quantum physics, which teaches that all things are complex, chaotic and uncertain.

Newtonian thinking suggests that there is one best way to get from A to B. Quantum thinking encourages people to think that there are many equally valid ways. Newtonian thinking stresses that any problem is best solved by breaking it into smaller parts and examining each part in turn. Quantum thinking encourages managers to look at the relationship between these parts.

Ms Zohar argues that Newtonian thinking is still prevalent in professions such as law, accountancy and finance, where rationality and analysis form the foundation for the way they are taught. Many senior managers come from these professions and most M&A external advisers are members of them. Consequently, the agenda followed in an M&A is likely to concentrate on hard management issues that can be resolved through Newtonian means. Yet the evidence is clear that it is the soft people issues that, if they are not resolved, will undermine the long-term viability of an M&A and which are least susceptible to black-and-white solutions.

Challenging the status quo or conventional wisdom is crucial in the process of testing the logic of an M&A and in achieving its creative potential. At IDEO, a California-based industrial design company that created the Polaroid I-Zone Camera and Crest Toothpaste's Neat Squeeze Tube, design teams are expected to make mistakes early and often – and team members are encouraged to question any and all assumptions about what innovation means. At IDEO, people are not deemed to be innovative unless they are challenging the client's, the team's and their own pre-existing notions.

This means that any notions other than standard company or industry orthodoxies are given an open hearing. David Kelly, IDEO's founder, argues that innovation is not just about surprising ideas but also about surprising people – and that fostering innovation is mainly about encouraging people to relate to each other in creative ways. "Being a design genius is great," he concludes. "Being a design genius at the expense of the team is not."

Stage three: collaboration

The move to higher synergies, described in Chapters 3 and 4, needs to be underpinned, not only by a change in team working but also in the relationship between line managers or supervisors and their staff.

Clifford Chance, a British law firm that merged with Pünder (Germany) and Rogers & Wells (America), is well aware that its goal to become a global law firm requires employees to share knowledge and learning and that this will only happen when traditional boundaries between legal and support staff are broken down. Paul Greenwood, director of knowledge and information, says:

> *Instead of the traditional division between lawyers and the back office, we are already seeing a "middle office" develop. From the lawyers' side, the middle office contains professional support lawyers who don't do transactional work but provide much of the necessary expertise and know-how. They will increasingly conduct post-transaction reviews to see where we can codify what we do and improve upon it. From the support staff, we will see new roles, for instance for information technology "hybrids" and for other interdisciplinary specialists.*

But if different groups of employees are to contribute in new ways, they must be confident that their efforts will be appreciated and not censured. The first step is to eliminate blame. A blame culture stifles risk-taking and discourages openness. People will not experiment because of the stigma attached to failure. Organisations often reinforce this fear when they promote a commitment to "error-free" work or announce a "zero tolerance for failure".

If managers want their staff to test out the germs of good ideas at work, they have to explicitly reassure them that there will be no comeback if anything goes wrong.

This was the conclusion of a study into risk-taking carried out by Fiona Lee, an assistant professor of psychology at the University of Michigan, who, with two academics from Harvard Business School, looked at how assumptions about the consequences of failure undermined a new IT initiative at a large mid-western health-care organisation.

The organisation had been created in the mid-1990s by merging five teaching hospitals, 30 health-care centres and 120 outpatient clinics. To help create an integrated management information system, the board introduced a website that would provide medical staff and administrators with a single access point for retrieving the most up-to-date clinical information. There was no formal training course for the system, so employees had to experiment to learn how to use it to best effect.

In a survey of 688 staff covering all work units in the newly formed organisation, Ms Lee and her colleagues assessed how each person used the technology and how this use was influenced by the management culture in their work units. She found that individuals were more willing to experiment with the new system – trying out different software applications and testing new system features – when their departmental managers did two things: stated explicitly that making mistakes would be okay, and refrained from punishing employees' errors.

Managers who gave mixed signals, such as verbally encouraging experimentation while keeping in place a reward system that punished failure, created mistrust and confusion. The effect of inconsistent messages was particularly strong among junior staff. Medical students, for example, assumed that failed experiments could harm their careers because of the need to win advancement. By contrast, Ms Lee found that employees who were "allowed the room to fail" ended up being the most proficient and satisfied with the new technology, as well as the quickest to integrate it into their everyday work.

The second step is to make fostering and championing staff creativity a core management task rather than a discretionary one. Casework on how ideas are shaped in organisations at Roffey Park Institute (and discussed further in *Successful Innovation* by Michel Syrett and Jean Lammiman[2]) suggests that managers can foster creativity in their staff in a number of ways (see Chart 9.2).

- They can act as "sponsors", promoting the idea inside the organisation, ensuring that it is not dismissed and sustaining interest during prolonged periods of gestation.
- They can act as "sounding boards", allowing the person with the idea to draw on their broader knowledge or impartial viewpoint to inform or validate the premise or to comment on the practicalities.
- As a member of a project development team or on a one-to-one basis, they can help "shape" the idea, fleshing out the premise or finding practical ways of making it "real".

Chart 9.2 **The principal roles in ideas development**

Role	Definition	Often undertaken by
Sparks	People who "spark" the creative process by spotting or coming up with the idea, creating the vision or defining the need	Anyone employed by or associated with the organisation; often comes from the least expected area
Sponsors	People who promote the idea or project inside the organisation, ensuring that it is not dismissed, and who sustain interest during difficult or lean times	Senior line managers, members of the board, non-executive directors
Shapers	People who make the idea or project "real", fleshing out the premise and/or finding practical means to meet its objectives	Members of the project team appointed to implement the idea, process-oriented consultants, R&D staff
Sounding boards	People outside the project whose objectivity and broader knowledge can be drawn on to inform and validate the premise or to comment on the practicalities	Informal or formal members of personal or professional networks, trusted colleagues, strategy-oriented consultants
Specialists	People who draw on their specialist knowledge or skills to shape the idea or project from a specific standpoint, often using the opportunity to break new ground in the field	Members of the project team, consultants (process and strategy), academics and researchers, R&D staff

Source: Roffey Park Institute, 2000

◪ Lastly, they can use their own specialist knowledge – for example, in technology, law or finance – to underpin its implementation or provide a particular perspective.

The third step is to ensure that whatever knowledge, insights or ideas emerge from individual work units are shared throughout the whole organisation. With the blurring of boundaries between organisations and the reduced expectations of security among younger sections of the workforce, this process – in contrast to the two others described above – in newly merged organisations is beginning to resemble that which took place in the strategic alliances of the 1990s.

Lufthansa played a leading role in setting up the Star Alliance in 1995 – consisting of itself and United Airlines in America, Scandinavian Airlines (SAS), Varig in Brazil, Air Canada and Thai Airlines – the largest of all airline alliances in terms of the number of companies involved. The Star Alliance has no central authority. In terms of soft issues such as customer service and relationship marketing, the strength of the network depends on its weakest link. There is no obvious mechanism for the stronger members like Lufthansa to exert pressure on the weaker ones. Any improvement has to be achieved through sharing experience and best practice.

Lufthansa had already gained valuable experience in "borderless learning" in the early 1990s, when the company had outsourced support functions such as check-in services, aircraft maintenance and food service. Surveys indicate that these services account for two-thirds of customers' flight satisfaction. So managers at Lufthansa have to provide what they call "network glue": seamless transnational structures to develop a global outlook in all staff and inspire the right level of customer service from the "absent ones" (staff not employed by Lufthansa but who perform important tasks on the company's behalf).

Drawing on this experience, Thomas Sattelberger, human-resources director, planned a series of programmes and events designed not only to instil an "alliance mentality" among staff from different members of the Star Alliance, but also to encourage them to share their knowledge and experience. These include international road shows to communicate the ideas and vision of the Alliance, cross-cultural workshops, and joint management-development programmes designed specifically to encourage executives from all member companies to work together in developing new strategies.

Mr Sattelberger feels strongly that individuals only contribute their own insights and experience when they identify with the aims of the enterprise. He uses the word "feel" time and again when describing the task of creating a common identity among employees from different member companies:

> I can look at myself in many ways. I feel Bavarian because I am a citizen of Bavaria. I feel German because I have German nationality. I feel European because my country is part of the European Union. In the same way, managers and employees in the new initiative are asking themselves whether they are part of, for example, Lufthansa Cargo, Lufthansa or the Star Alliance. The key question for us is how we can create a common sense of identity and purpose and therefore a willingness to share our expertise – and to do so among flight attendants in Chicago, purchasing agents in India and maintenance staff in Beijing.

Planning back to the future

The merger boom of recent years has been driven by a belief in size, commercial muscle and economies of scale. In industries where integration and consolidation are imperative, mergers and acquisitions are like lightening: they strike the same house more than once. Only eight years separated the merger of SmithKline and Beecham and the merger of the newly created company with Glaxo. And not so long ago there were the Big Eight accounting firms; now there are the Big Five, which as a result of the fallout from the collapse of Enron may become the Big Four.

In terms of sustaining innovation, this means that the processes and initiatives that preserved a creative capability in any one partner in the merger need to stay in place on an almost continuous basis. A good example is the means an organisation takes to preserve its corporate "memory".

New technologies – intranets, discussional databases or some other form of electronic brainstorming or videoconferencing software – have made it possible to record the process of successful innovation in "real time". Recording the steps and use of analogy and metaphor that led to creative breakthroughs in the past, without the retrospective filtering of hindsight, can be of powerful assistance to innovation in newly merged companies. Just as a good scientist records every stage of every experiment for personal or historical posterity, so a company database can provide current employees with an insight or understanding of what sparked the innovative processes of previous teams.

There are also the individuals responsible for past innovations who may either choose or be forced to leave the organisation during the merger process. They do not cease to exist. If, as is increasingly the case, they do not choose to work full-time for a competitor, their expertise can be used on a freelance or consultancy basis to inform or advise current employees charged with following through the original idea. This, of course, presupposes that exit processes are handled with sensitivity and tact.

The importance of using mergers as a launch pad for sustainable innovation cannot be overstated. The workforce expect change and, provided they are reassured that their future is secure, will not question initiatives that would be resisted in periods of stable commercial cruising. Speaking at a seminar at London Business School, Steve Wilson, Diageo's brand innovation leader, described how the introduction of a radical new decision-making process, StageGate, helped the company reassess the market demand for popular spirits brands such as Smirnoff and J&B by producing ready-mixed cocktails that could be bought over the counter.

The StageGate process is based on a series of meetings where new concepts are (respectively) developed, assessed and allocated the finance by managers empowered to make decisions on the spot. Mr Wilson concluded:

> This was a radical break with the way we made decisions in the past. We were able to set it in place because the merger between Grand Metropolitan and Guinness provided us with a clean slate from which to work. I doubt we would have been able to do it in either company prior to the merger.

Summary

Below is a list of the main points in each chapter of the book.

Fusion and fission

- M&As are driven as much by human impulse as by sound business sense.
- M&As involve combining both physical and intellectual assets.
- M&As rarely improve shareholder value.
- Business performance often plummets after a merger.
- Business managers often judge the success of an M&A by different criteria from those used by, say, academics or analysts, and are upbeat about the value of mergers and acquisitions.

Magnetic attraction

- How well the courtship is handled can have a decisive influence on the success of a merger.
- Managers should focus on building relationships with their counterparts in the other firm before they enter formal negotiations.
- Human-resources managers should be included in merger discussions to ensure that people issues are not overlooked.
- Intermediaries play an important role but should not be allowed to drive merger negotiations.
- Constructive dialogue requires both merger teams to disclose commercial, cultural and personal information that helps build an accurate and realistic picture of their businesses.

Analysing the atoms

- Due diligence should not be treated as a stand-alone process, performed by legal and financial experts, and heavily concentrated on physical assets. It should give as much weight to the intellectual and emotional capital of a business.
- Due diligence is typically conducted primarily by legal, financial and commercial specialists who often attach little importance to the courtship process. The due diligence team should contain human-resources specialists and other professionals who have a greater understanding of the relational nuances of the potential link-up.
- Every component of due diligence should be designed around the

M&A's source of potential synergy or strategic leverage, then subdivided into a set of critical success factors.

- Due diligence can unleash a maelstrom of detail. The merger team must retain a tenacious grip on the original vision and goals and keep communicating these to their prospective partner and the due diligence teams.
- Merger teams must act as visionaries and strategic sponsors. They must be able to make their decisions based on a blend of analysis and intuition.

Creating a new nucleus

- Merger success is clearly linked to effective integration planning before the M&A takes place.
- Integration should be viewed as a unique opportunity to change the climate, culture and working practices of the new business as the merger takes place.
- Managers often go into crisis mode and design integration processes that are piecemeal or place too much reliance on project-management disciplines.
- People-based mergers need people-based integration processes that are collaborative in their design and implementation.
- The employees involved in the integration can become the "positively charged" nucleus of the merged business.

Explosions and implosions

- The announcement of an M&A sends shock waves through both organisations that must be responded to immediately in order to prevent a deterioration of morale and performance.
- Communication processes can help establish the values and vision of the merged company, and create a climate that encourages people to work together.
- The M&A announcement must be meticulously planned so that all concerned supply consistent messages about the merger.
- The managers of an acquired business need support and can play a valuable role in encouraging their employees to collaborate.
- Merger celebrations can be a cathartic experience and help all concerned to let go of the past and brace themselves for change.

Minimising the fallout

- The strain of the immediate transition can weaken the capacity of the newly combined business to grow through innovation and creativity.

◪ The performance of the combined business can plummet unless active steps are taken to combat "merger syndrome".

◪ Losing talented people can undermine employees' confidence in the new business and encourage cultural entrenchment.

◪ Financial incentives are a necessary but not a sufficient means of motivating skilled employees.

◪ There are a number of practical steps managers should take to help employees resolve their individual problems and play an active part in shaping the emerging organisation.

Stirring the electrons

◪ Line managers are often a neglected resource during an M&A, but they can make an important contribution.

◪ Their chief role is to help ensure that statements about collaboration and synergy are translated into constructive, everyday working experiences.

◪ They are uniquely positioned to build trust among employees by ensuring that difficult changes are implemented as professionally as possible.

◪ Line managers can act as "change barometers", giving valuable feedback to integration managers about how well employees are adjusting to the merger.

◪ Line managers are often best placed to encourage valued employees who might otherwise leave during the immediate transition.

Achieving fusion

◪ M&As provide a rare opportunity to introduce across-the-board measures that will foster innovation.

◪ The emphasis should be on measures that will change the way problems and opportunities are assessed and decisions are made.

◪ "Disruptives" should be given more licence to question black-and-white thinking and follow up hunches: cross-functional teams and integration projects should include "intuitives" and behaviouralists able to tackle the soft issues, as well as analytical rationalists capable of dealing with the hard issues.

◪ Any post-merger initiatives should support and sustain the "corporate memory" of the organisation so that future staff can access the creative thinking that led to past innovations.

Notes and references

Chapter 1

1 Dealogic produces *M&A Review*, a free publication that provides a monthly summary of global M&A activity. To receive an e-mail copy, contact mareview@dealogic.com

2 "Lessons from master acquirers: a CEO roundtable on making mergers succeed", *Harvard Business Review*, May–June 2000.

3 Extract from a speech given by Steve Case to investors during the "AOL Time Warner Investor Day", January 30th 2001.

4 Quote from "The culture will take care of itself", *Business Week*, June 1999.

5 Quote from "Reed: reflections on a culture clash", *Fortune*, March 27th 2000.

6 Quote from a case study by Wendy Hirsh in Devine, M. and Hirsh, W., *Mergers and Acquisitions: getting the people bit right*, Roffey Park Institute, UK, October 1998.

7 Case study of Halifax and Leeds merger by Marion Devine, included in *Mergers and Acquisitions: getting the people bit right*, op. cit.

8 Syrett, M. and Lammiman, J., *Successful Innovation*, Profile Books: The Economist Books, 2002.

Chapter 2

1 "Quest for bigness drives urge to merge", *Across the Board*, May 16th 2001, The Conference Board.

2 *Unleasing value in the new economy*, report published by Andersen, 2000.

3 "Don't believe the hype", *Investors Chronicle*, 26th January 2001.

4 *Making mergers work for profitable growth*, report by Mercer Management Consulting.

5 *Creating value from acquisition integration*, PA Consulting, 2000.

6 *Creating shareholder value through mergers and acquisitions*, KPMG, 2001.

7 Unger, J., "The people trauma of major mergers", *Journal of Industrial Management*, Vol. 10, April 1986, p. 17.

8 Bleeke, J. and Isono, J.A., "Succeeding at cross-border mergers and acquisitions", *McKinsey Quarterly*, 3, 1990.

9 "Strategic perspectives on European cross-border acquisitions: the views from top European executives", *European Management*, Vol. 15, No. 4, August 1997.

10 Ingham, H., Kran, I. and Lovestam, A., "Mergers and profitability: a managerial success story?", *Journal of Management Studies*, 29:2, March 1992.

11 "Lessons from master acquirers: a CEO roundtable on making mergers succeed", *Harvard Business Review*, May–June 2000.

12 Kitching, J., "Winning and losing with European acquisitions", *Harvard Business Review*, March–April 1974.

Chapter 3

1 *American business leaders*, a report published by Deloitte & Touche, 1996.

2 "Mind the culture gap", *Sunday Telegraph*, June 17th 2001.

3 *People implications of mergers and acquisitions, joint ventures and divestments*, survey report by the Chartered Institute of Personnel and Development in association with PricewaterhouseCoopers and Bacon and Woodrow, September 2000.

4 *Employee communications during merger*, Report No. 1270-00-R, The Conference Board, 2000.

5 "An interview with Glaxo Wellcome", *Lessons learned from mergers and acquisitions*, Right Management Consultants, 1999.

6 Case study on Bank of Ireland's acquisition of Bristol & West Building Society by Marion Devine on behalf of Roffey Park Institute.

7 These headings are used by Accenture in its *Blueprint for business integration* model and have been adapted for the purposes of this chapter.

8 Max Habeck is co-author with Fritz Kröger and Michael Träm of *After the merger*, published by Financial Times/Prentice Hall.

9 City Comment, Electronic *Telegraph*, July 6th 1999.

10 "Packing it in at home and abroad", *The Grocer*, June 16th 2001.

11 Devine, M. and Hirsh, W., *Mergers and Acquisitions: getting the people bit right*, Roffey Park Institute, 1998.

12 "Lessons from master acquirers: a CEO roundtable on making mergers succeed" *Harvard Business Review*, May–June 2000.

13 *BBC News*, May 4th 2001, news.bbc.co.uk

14 Hunt, J., *Mergers and acquisitions*, London Business School and Egon Zehnder International, 1987.

Chapter 4

1 *The Economist*, October 25th 2000, page 26.
2 Information kindly provided by Sheena McCaffrey, a solicitor specialising in employment legislation.
3 *Watson Wyatt's Worldwide 1988/99 Mergers and Acquisitions Survey*, Watson Wyatt Consultants, 1999.
4 Rankine, D., *Commercial Due Diligence: A Guide to Reducing Risk in Acquisitions*, Financial Times Prentice Hall, UK, 1999.
5 Thomson, K., *Emotional Capital*, Capstone, 1998.
6 Kay, I. and Shelton, M., "The people problem in mergers", *McKinsey Quarterly*, No. 4, 2000.
7 Hampden-Turner, C. and Trompenaars, F., *Building Cross-Cultural Competence*, Wiley, 2000.
8 "Mind the culture gap", *Sunday Telegraph*, June 17th 2001.
9 *Lesson learned from mergers and acquisitions: best practices in workforce integration*, Right Management Consultants, 1999.

Chapter 5

1 "Making the deal real: how GE Capital integrates acquisitions", *Harvard Business Review*, January–February 1998.
2 Gates, S., *Performance measures during merger and acquisition integration*, Research Report 1274, The Conference Board, 2000.
3 Marks, M.L. and Mirvis, P., "Managing mergers, acquisitions and alliances: creating an effective transition structure", *Organisational Dynamics*, Winter 2000.
4 Marks, M.L. and Mirvis, P., op. cit.
5 Gates, S., op. cit.
6 *Harvard Business Review*, op. cit.
7 *Creating shareholder value from acquisition integration*, PA Consulting Group, 2000.

Chapter 6

1 Extract from a case-study on the Halifax Building Society prepared for Roffey Park Institute by Marion Devine.
2 Hanson, P., *The M&A Transition Guide*, John Wiley & Sons, 2001.
3 Schweiger, D. and Weber, Y., "Strategies for managing human resources during mergers and acquisitions: an empirical investigation", *Human Resource Planning*, Vol. 12, No. 2, 1989.
4 *Wall Street Journal*, May 5th 2000.

Chapter 7

1 Angwin, D., *The dynamics of post-acquisition management*, Warwick Business School, 1996.
2 Marks, M.L. and Mirvis, P., "Merger syndrome: stress and uncertainty", *Mergers & Acquisitions*, Summer 1995.
3 Bekier, M., Bogardus, A. and Oldham, T., "Why mergers fail", *McKinsey Quarterly*, No. 1, 2001.
4 *The Economist*, December 14th 2000.
5 *The Economist*, February 1st 2001.
6 *The Economist*, February 1st 2001.
7 *Lessons learned from mergers and acquisitions*, Right Management Consultants, 1999.
8 "Barriers to acculturation in mergers and acquisitions: strategic human resource implications", *Journal of European Business Education*, Vol. 2, No. 2, May 1993.
9 Right Management Consultants, op. cit.
10 KPMG, *Unlocking shareholder value: the keys to success*, 1999.
11 Devine M., Garrow, V., Hirsh, W. and Holbeche, L., *Strategic alliances: getting the people bit right*, Roffey Park Institute, 2000.
12 *The Economist*, July 13th 2000.
13 *Playing to win: strategic rewards in the war for talent, fifth annual report*, Watson Wyatt, 2000/2001.
14 *Magnetic attraction: the potential of talent and the corporate brand*, Stanton Marris, June 2001.
15 Marks, M.L. and Mirvis, P., "Managing mergers, acquisitions and alliances: creating an effective transition structure", *Organisational Dynamics*, Winter 2000.
16 Right Management Consultants, op. cit.
17 Devine, M. and Lammiman, J., "Original Synergy", *People Management*, April 2000.

Chapter 8

1 Devine, M., *Roffey Park M&A checklist: a guide to effective people management during a merger or acquisition*, Roffey Park Institute, 1999.
2 Marks, M.L. and Mirvis, P., "Rebuilding after the merger: dealing with survivor sickness", *Organisational Dynamics*, Autumn 1992.
3 Nonaka, I., "A Dynamic Theory of Organizational Knowledge Creation", *Organization Science*, Vol. 5-1, February 1994.
4 Inkpen, A., "Learning, knowledge acquisition and strategic

alliances", *European Management Journal*, Vol. 16, No. 2, April 1998.

5   Devine, M., Garrow, V., Hirsh, W. and Holbeche, L., *Strategic alliances: getting the people bit right*, Roffey Park Institute, 2000.

6   Davis, R., "Compatibility in corporate marriages", *Harvard Business Review*, 46, 1968.

7   Harrison, R. and Stokes, H., *Diagnosing your Organisation's Culture*, Harrison & Associates Inc, 1990.

8   Deal, T. and Kennedy, A., *Corporate Cultures*, Addison-Wesley, 1982.

9   Hall, W., *Managing Cultures*, John Wiley & Sons, 1995.

Chapter 9

1   Lutz, R., *Guts: the Seven Laws of Business That Made Chrysler the World's Hottest Car Company*, John Wiley & Sons, 1998.

2   Syrett, M. and Lammiman, J., *Successful Innovation*, Profile Books: The Economist Books, 2002.

Appendix

M&A research surveys and reports

American business leaders, Deloitte & Touche, 1996.

Beyond the headlines: a survey of lessons learned from merger and acquisition activity, Andersen Consulting, 2000.

Creating shareholder value from acquisition integration, PA Consulting and University of Edinburgh Management School, 2000.

Employee communications during mergers, The Conference Board, Research Report 1270-00-R, 2000.

Lessons learned from mergers and acquisitions, Right Management Consultants, 1999.

Making mergers work for profitable growth, Mercer Management Consultancy, 2000.

Mergers and acquisitions, John Hunt, London Business School and Egon Zehnder, 1987.

Mergers and acquisitions: getting the people bit right, Marion Devine and Wendy Hirsh, Roffey Park Institute, 1998.

People implications of mergers and acquisitions, joint ventures and divestments, Chartered Institute of Personnel and Development, in association with PricewaterhouseCoopers and Bacon and Woodrow, 2000.

Performance measurement during merger and acquisition integration, Stephen Gates, The Conference Board, Research Report 1274-00-RR, 2000.

Realising the value of acquisitions: a comparative study of European post-acquisition integration practices, PA Consulting Group, 2001.

Roffey Park M&A checklist: a guide to effective people management during a merger or acquisition, Marion Devine, Roffey Park Institute, Horsham, UK, 1999.

Strategic alliances: getting the people bit right, Marion Devine, Valerie Garrow, Wendy Hirsh, Linda Holbeche, Roffey Park Institute, Horsham, UK, 2000.

Unleashing value in the new economy, Andersen Consulting, 2000.

Watson Wyatt's worldwide 1998/99 mergers and acquisitions survey, Watson Wyatt Consultants, 1999.

Index